MW00633086

TALIA FUHRMAN

Desserts to live for

ghp

Gift of Health Press

Publisher Contact:
Gift of Health Press
Flemington, NJ 08822
for wholesale inquires please call:
1-800-474-WELL (9355)

Printed in United States of America
ISBN: 978-0-9992235-8-1

Library of Congress Control Number: 2021931179

WWW.TALIAFUHRMAN.COM

ACKNOWLEDGMENTS

I'd like to thank Jenna Fuhrman for graphics and copy writing, Mary Becker for recipe reviewing and testing, Linda Popescu for nutrition facts data, Eileen Murphy for copy writing, Tim Shay and Kyle Fidel for graphics work, Lauren Russell for organizing and Doris (Dee) Walfield for editing. I'd also like to thank my incredible support system of family and friends who encouraged me to pursue my passions of nutrition, healthy recipe creation and food photography.

ALSO BY TALIA FUHRMAN

LOVE YOUR BODY

In *Love Your Body*, Talia Fuhrman's first book, she shows readers how to get their green juice on, find their ideal weight, and get radiant, clear skin—and also how to gain confidence, enjoy strong friendships, and explore the passions that make them whole.

Motivated by her own struggles, and those of her friends—weight gain, skin troubles, stomach aches, frequent sickness, migraines—Talia knows that eating a plant-based diet packed with all-natural, nutrient-rich ingredients makes body issues a thing of the past. With a fresh, engaging voice, Talia inspires readers to nourish their mental and emotional health too. She places a strong emphasis on inner beauty, and offers advice on how to maximize their social lives, and care about the world around them through both healthy lifestyle practices and eco-conscious living tips.

With science-packed nutrition facts, actionable advice, and delicious recipes, this mind-body manual offers a fun, simple roadmap to a vegan lifestyle, and proves that loving your body—inside and out—can be positively delicious!

Table of Contents

A COOKBOOK BY TALIA FUHRMAN

DESSERTS TO LIVE FOR

BY TALIA FUHRMAN

FOR THE REST OF YOUR LIFE, USING THIS BOOK AS YOUR TOOL, YOU CAN "EAT YOUR CAKE" AND STAY HEALTHY TOO.

ENJOY GOOD HEALTH

If you, like me, possess a sweet tooth as large as your savory tooth, you can enjoy heavenly desserts with zero guilt, zero sacrifice and zero risk of bodily harm when the desserts you eat are made with only good-for-you ingredients. For the rest of your life, using this book as your tool, you can "eat your cake" and stay healthy too. Unlike most dessert recipes, every recipe in this unique, health-promoting book is sweetened with nothing but fruit and dried fruit! That means "the fruit and nothing but the fruit."

All harmful ingredients in conventional desserts, such as sugar, and other concentrated sweeteners, refined flour, butter, oil, dairy-based creams and artificial anything are excluded from these tasty recipes! Looking for gluten-free sweets? You will find a plethora of options here! Get ready to begin a revolutionary culinary journey that will protect your health, increase your nutritional knowledge and improve your skills in the kitchen. You will find a large variety of recipes from cookies, brownies and blondies to beautiful cakes, pies and ice creams within these pages. Some of the recipes call for overnight prep. I've labeled those recipes with a half moon graphic on the prep time.

SWEET TO THE CORE

First, let's take a knowledge dive into why processed sugar, sweeteners and other ingredients commonly used in desserts are so bad for us. This knowledge is extremely important as the average American consumes 150-170 pounds of sugar a year. Knowing the science will help you choose healthier desserts forever—especially when you discover how delicious they can taste.

Sugar is more dangerous than we thought in the past, as are many commonly used so-called "healthier" sugar replacements, such as maple syrup, agave nectar, honey and coconut sugar.

Sweeteners commonly viewed as "healthy" alternatives are processed the same way in the body as sugar and can cause the same serious health problems sugar does!

COMPOSITION OF SWEETENERS

All of these sweeteners are rapidly absorbed into the bloodstream and significantly contribute to the development of obesity, diabetes, heart disease and cancer. Despite their reputation as healthier alternatives to table sugar, natural sweeteners like agave nectar, honey and maple syrup are just as addictive and they do the same harm because they flood the bloodstream with glucose or fructose! The reality is that all concentrated sweeteners add substantial sugar calories to the diet while contributing very little nutritional value.

It is a common assumption that maple syrup is a healthier alternative to table sugar, but it contains 96 percent sucrose, so it is compositionally very similar to sugar. Coconut sugar contains 70-80 percent sucrose, and honey contains about 50 percent fructose and 45 percent glucose. Sucrose is half fructose and half glucose. It's composed of one fructose molecule linked to one glucose molecule. Agave nectar is about 80 percent fructose; it is almost the same as high-fructose corn syrup. All of these sweeteners promote weight gain and fat storage on the body.

The general rule is that all high-calorie, low-nutrient sweeteners have approximately the same effects on the body regardless of the ratio of glucose to fructose or what type of plant they come from. There is nothing innocent about it. No matter how good those sugar-loaded desserts look or taste, they can slowly kill us with a life-shortening disease if we consume them on a regular basis throughout our lives.

HONEY

Just like sugar, the nutrients in honey are insignificant. Add this to the fact that honey is highly concentrated fructose and glucose and that puts additional stress on the body, especially our liver and kidneys. There are 64 calories in one tablespoon of honey and all of these calories are in the form of concentrated sugar. Websites on the Internet claim that honey is nutritious and contains antioxidants and minerals like calcium, iron, magnesium, manganese, phosphorus, potassium and zinc; however, the reality is that the quantity of these nutrients in honey is insignificant (practically nil) compared to the quantity in real fruits and vegetables.

Upon researching the vitamin and mineral content in a serving of honey, it becomes obvious that claims asserting that honey is high in these minerals and vitamins like B6, thiamin, niacin and riboflavin are false. Honey, whether raw or cooked, is almost all sugar and no fiber. Fiber slows down the rate of carbohydrate absorption from the small intestine, delaying the after-meal flow of glucose into the blood.

Without fiber, glucose is absorbed rapidly. A surge of glucose into the bloodstream at a rapid rate leads to an insulin spike. The more insulin spikes we have, the greater our likelihood of developing type II diabetes, heart attacks and its associated cardiovascular problems as well as breast, colon and prostate cancer. Excessive insulin also increases fat storage and the risk of cancer.

AGAVE NECTAR

Agave nectar, or agave syrup, is used widely as a sweetener in so-called healthy food products from breakfast bars to cereals to vegan ice creams. It has become the sweetener used by health-conscious folks who want to avoid sugar, high-fructose corn syrup, and artificial sweeteners. There is enthusiasm about it for having a seemingly low glycemic index, which would make it a friendly sugar substitute for those with diabetes.

Unfortunately, these enthusiasts are misguided. What agave nectar does have is a lot of fructose. Actually, it has more fructose than high-fructose corn syrup! It's refined and processed just like high-fructose corn syrup. Agave nectar is between 55-97 percent fructose, depending on the brand, while high-fructose corn syrup averages 55 percent fructose. Pretty shocking, right?

To be fair, before processing and refinement, agave nectar was once in a natural form, albeit a high-in-fructose natural form. Before manufacturing and standard practices of refinement, true agave nectar comes from the Blue Agaves (also known as tequila agave plants) that thrive in the volcanic soils of Southern Mexico. However, the agave nectar we buy in stores is a far cry from the agave nectar that comes from the natural plant. Most "agave" is nothing more than a laboratory-generated, highly-compacted fructose syrup.

Although processing methods may vary among manufacturers, commercially available agave is converted into a fructose-rich syrup using genetically modified enzymes and a chemically intensive process employing the use of caustic acids, clarifiers, and filtration chemicals.

After all of this processing, agave nectar generally contains upwards of 80 percent fructose, completely wreaking havoc on our health, our skin quality, and if we eat it often enough, our weight. Fructose may even be worse than glucose because it doesn't just increase insulin levels, it increases our insulin resistance in ways that glucose doesn't, which increases the likelihood of type 2 diabetes. Our bodies metabolize fructose in the liver in the same manner in which we metabolize alcohol. Just as excess alcohol inclines us to developing a fat "beer belly," excess fructose makes us prone to developing a fat "fructose belly."

Every time you imagine sinking your teeth into a cupcake sweetened with agave, think "fructose belly." That should get you to put that cupcake down.

MAPLE SYRUP

Maple syrup is similar to honey and agave nectar because it is just concentrated sugar calories and low in nutrients and fiber too. Continual exposure to low-nutrient, low-fiber, high-calorie sweeteners dulls our taste buds to the natural sweet taste of whole fruits. If your aim is to stay at a healthy weight and not get a life-threatening disease cutting your life short, these liquid sweeteners are best avoided. Just like pure sugar, maple syrup is also linked to increased risks of weight gain, diabetes, heart disease and cancers, because it is sugar.

WHY SHARP MINDS AND SUGAR DON'T MIX

In life, no brain, no gain! So, of course, we want our brain to be as sharp as possible. Understanding how chronic sugar consumption leads to both short-term and long-term decreased mental functioning is critically important. The effects are striking!

Sugar travels through the blood-brain barrier quickly and wreaks havoc with brain cells.

Blood vessels all over our bodies become inflamed when we consume too much sugar, and this includes the blood vessels in our brains which leads to a progressive decline in brain function. [1,2]

Deficits in learning, memory, motor speed and other cognitive functions have been found in studies on those who have diabetes.[3] However, even for those without diabetes, greater sugar consumption is associated with similar damage, demonstrated by lower scores on tests of cognitive function, reduction in memory and attention, and higher risk of dementia with aging. It is not only the heightened blood sugar, but also its effect to raise insulin resistance. Higher consumption of commercial baked goods containing white flour and sugar also raises blood pressure and cholesterol.[4,5]

SUGAR ADDICTION IS REAL

Not only can sugar make us depressed and harm our cognitive capacities, but it can be as addictive as drugs.[6] Sweets are associated with binging, craving, withdrawal symptoms, and sensitization of the same brain pathway as addiction to amphetamines, narcotics and alcohol. For many, sugar addiction could be an even harder habit to break, because the damage is so gradual, insidious and widespread that people don't recognize its harm.

White flour is essentially the same as sugar as it is converted into sugar during digestion and absorbed as sugar into the blood stream. The same harm also occurs when we consume other sweetening agents such as maple syrup, honey, agave nectar and coconut sugar, our dopamine receptors begin to down-regulate, leading to fewer receptors for the dopamine to latch onto.

Every single time we consume foods with large amounts of free sugar (sugar missing its fiber) our dopamine receptors become further desensitized and then greater amounts of sugar are required to produce the same stimulatory effects. This is typical of what happens with any addiction, from heroin to cigarettes. More junk food is necessary over time to achieve the same level of reward. People who are more susceptible to forming addictions are at a greater risk of developing a sugar addiction and losing control with calorie intake, just as they are at a greater risk of alcohol and drug addiction. It is a serious problem for millions of Americans.

MORE SUGAR AND MORE HEART ATTACKS AND CANCERS

According to the epic 2014 JAMA Internal Medicine study, which followed over 40,000 people for 15 years, the link between sugar and heart disease holds true even for people at healthy weights and regardless of age, gender and physical activity level.[7] Participants who consumed 25 percent or more calories each day from processed sugar were more than twice as likely to die from heart disease than those whose diets included less than 10 percent added sugar.

This includes the agave nectar, maple syrup, honey and coconut sugar you see in "healthy" desserts at the vegan restaurants and in health food stores across the country. What's striking about the study is that how many fruits and veggies participants ate was irrelevant! "Regardless of their Healthy Eating Index scores, people who ate more processed sugar still had higher cardiovascular mortality," reported Dr. Teresa Fung, adjunct professor of nutrition at the Harvard School of Public Health. Previous studies have demonstrated that excess sugar can raise blood pressure and stimulate the liver to dump more harmful fats into the bloodstream. It's disturbing that we've known that the majority of human cancers are preventable via diet and nutrition since the 1960s when the World Health Organization began examining diet and lifestyle factors and came to these conclusions. Data since then has come to the same verdicts and even more compelling evidence continues to mount that high-sugar, high-meat, low-fiber and low-nutrient diets, the very diets of most Americans are what leads to the majority of cancer cases in the United States.

Every major scientific health organization in the United States, including the National Cancer Society, the American Cancer Society, and the Department of Health and Human Services, supports research findings that diet and cancer are intertwined and these organizations have presented dietary suggestions for the public in hopes of engendering greater awareness.

When sugar combines with other low-nutrient, low-fiber foods in our environment, like white flour and oils, the very ingredients found in most dessert recipes, we have essentially created a cancer cake. Those sweets and treats everywhere, from Starbucks to supermarkets, are actually the perfect formula for cancer and heart disease to develop later in life.

WHY PROCESSED SUGARY SWEETS, WHITE FLOUR AND CHILDREN SHOULD NOT MEET

Exposure to negative and toxic influences when we are young has the greatest influence on whether or not we will get cancer or heart disease as older adults. Here's the lowdown on why.

"In adults, our valuable genetic material (DNA) is wound up in a tight ball, like the rubber bands on the inside of a golf ball. When we are young and cells are replicating and growing, the DNA unwinds, exposing more of its surface. This makes it more susceptible to damage from toxic exposure. According to the U.S. Environmental Protection Agency, infants and toddlers have a ten times greater cancer risk than adults when exposed to gene-damaging chemicals. In a similar manner, an unhealthy diet can do substantially more damage to a young body than to an adult one. The earlier in life, the greater the potential for damage." ~ Joel Fuhrman M.D., Disease-Proof Your Child, page 79

Breast cancer is associated with a high body weight and now we also know that white flour, sugar and too much animal product consumption are all associated with breast cancer too. Interestingly though is that body weight during the twenty years prior to the time we receive a cancer diagnosis is not as dangerous as being overweight as a child or teenager.

This isn't to say that gaining weight at later stages of life is not harmful, but it does mean that childhood and teenage exposure to toxins, sweetened desserts and junk food plays a more critical role in whether or not cancer will happen in our 60s, 70s, 80s and beyond. Cancer in the body is established over a period of decades.[8]

Ironically, it's usually in our younger years that we take our health for granted and don't care as much about the effects, for better or worse, of what we eat. Sugar and its syrupy sweetener cousins are unquestionably dangerous when consumed as youngsters when more of the surface of our DNA is exposed. Studies conducted on animals have confirmed this same principle, that eating nutritiously early in life plays a more critical role in whether or not we end up with a chronic, painful or deadly disease decades down the road.[9]

KIDS LOVE HEALTHY FOOD

I'm sure you'll find that the desserts in this book are amazingly delicious. There is an abundance of recipes to choose from, so you can experiment and find your own favorites and kids can find their own favorites too. Desserts sweetened with fruit can taste sensational and this book is a testament to that.

We have a tremendous advantage in that we were designed to love the taste of natural foods. This is especially true for kids. Our genes are engineered to like fruits without any trickery, forcing or coaxing. We didn't possess the plethora of junk foods surrounding us when we were evolving. Our taste buds haven't changed even a little bit in thousands of years. Not only do kids love the taste of natural plant foods, but if fed properly they will learn to reject the overpowering tastes of junk foods all on their own. I am a testament of this principle myself.

Growing up, I watched my dad lecture children in my classes, at his office and in health conferences around the country. I saw how my peers reacted to what he taught about nutrition; they were always curious, intrigued and eager to eat healthfully. When provided with accurate information, they loved soaking it up like sponges, ready for more answers. They wished to know what I knew and wanted their parents to feed them the foods my parents fed me. I've noticed that kids are often the most excited to eat healthfully out of any age group! Growing up, my friends didn't assume that junk foods were more delicious like many of the adults I speak with today do. The difference in attitudes between children and adults raised on the standard American diet can be striking. Children are often better at rejecting junk foods than adults. All of my younger siblings are testaments of these words too.

My siblings and I were raised in the same home in the same town with the same ubiquity of junk foods outside of the house, at school and our friends' houses. My parents used the same strategy to raise all four of us. All of my siblings and I love the Nutritarian (nutrient-dense, plant-rich) lifestyle we grew up on and we will be sticking to it for the rest of our lives. We all tried junk foods too; my parents didn't control how we ate at friends' homes. They taught us the importance of eating healthy foods, but respected us enough to let us make our own choices outside of our home. We got to know what conventional foods tasted like, desserts and all and we all felt the same way ~ grateful for the healthy foods we were brought up on and wholeheartedly prefer them.

WHY WHOLE FRUITS ARE SUPERIOR

What makes whole fruits different than extracted sweeteners is that they are packed with fiber to regulate the entrance of glucose, fructose and sucrose into our bodies, and they are loaded with phytonutrients and polyphenols to buffer the effects of the natural sugars inside the fruit. Furthermore, the fructose and glucose threshold is much lower in fruits. Fruit only contains a few grams of fructose per serving and do not expose us to enough fructose to trigger fat storage, unless we consume an overabundance of fruit juice or dried fruit.

DATES ARE THE CHOSEN ONE

My main sweetener of choice in this book is dates. You too will fall in love with dates as there are magical qualities in dates that make them the perfect sweetener for healthy, anti-cancer, heart disease-fighting dessert recipes! Dates are unique for quite a few reasons. They are particularly sweet for their small size.

Wouldn't such a high-sugar food raise blood sugar and triglycerides, increase oxidative stress on our bodies and incline us to gain weight? Not at all. Dates also happen to be loaded with fiber and phytonutrients and this makes all the difference in the world. Just like other whole fruits jam-packed with fiber and phytochemicals, the nutrients and fiber in dates buffer the effects of those natural sugars.

There are no documented adverse effects of consuming a reasonable amount of dates on blood sugar or weight. Quite the contrary, studies show beneficial improvements in triglycerides and antioxidant levels upon consuming dates regularly![10]

IMPORTANT DATE NUTRITION FACTS:

1) Dates are packed with polyphenols, and in particular, a type of polyphenol called tannins.[11] Polyphenols are a class of antioxidants with incredible health-protecting properties.

2) The fiber content of dates is between 6.4-11.5% depending on the variety and degree of ripeness. Fiber is known for its ability to lower cholesterol and fight obesity, heart disease and colorectal cancer. The primary fiber in dates is insoluble fiber, which binds to fat and cholesterol and carries it out of the body.

3) There are at least 15 minerals in dates in significant quantities, including potassium, boron, calcium, cobalt, copper, iron, magnesium, manganese, phosphorous and zinc. Selenium is another element found in dates, which has been found to prevent cancer and increase immune system strength.

4) Dates contain protein: 23 different amino acids, many of which are not present in more popular fruits like oranges, apples and bananas.

5) Dates contain important vitamins including vitamin C, thiamine (vitamin B1), riboflavin (vitamin B2), niacin (vitamin B3), vitamin K and vitamin A. The B vitamins help with the metabolism of food and the formation of new blood cells.

Remember that it is the high-fiber and high-micronutrient content of fruits that helps protect us against cancer and heart disease.

A TRICK I USE IN BAKING WITH DATES

Usually the dates I purchase are soft and ready for using in any recipe within these pages. However, some dates can firm up over time and if they've been in storage for a little while, they remain perfect for baking but may need some softening. To soften dates, pit them with a sharp knife and soak them in water overnight.

WHY ALL RECIPES CAN BE PREPARED OIL-FREE

Guess what food ingredient has almost no micronutrients whatsoever? Oils. Every type of oil! That's right, even olive oil and coconut oil have no notable levels of vitamins, minerals or phytochemicals. Not only are oils devoid of nutrients, they are loaded with calories. Every single type of oil on this planet has 120 calories per tablespoon, all of which come from fat. When you consume oil, it is absorbed rapidly and your body can store this type of fat effortlessly in your hips and belly in about 10 minutes. Eating oil is pretty much the reverse of liposuction, yet most of us use it as a major ingredient or cook with it on a daily basis. The average American currently consumes 300 to 500 calories from added oil every single day. This adds up to over 100,000 extra calories each year! Here's another equation:

**AN EXTRA 100 CALORIES FROM OIL EACH DAY =
100 EXTRA POUNDS OF FAT IN 10 YEARS**

It's not a huge deal to eat a bit of oil here and there if you eat an overall healthy diet and are physically active and slim, but this is not the case for most people. As many Americans continue to become overweight or obese, consuming extra calories from oil leads to additional health problems. This is not simply a matter of fitting into your skinny jeans—at the rate we eat oil, we're facing heightened risks of diabetes, cancer, or heart attacks: for every 200 calories of any food consumed beyond your basic needs each day, your long-term risk of cancer increases by 20 percent.[12]

Oils are processed foods—there are no oil trees! Oils are generally extracted from plants with a petroleum chemical such as hexane. When you chemically extract oil from a whole plant food (like olives, nuts, or seeds), you remove desirable nutrients and fibers and obtain a fragmented food that contains little more than empty calories.

Of course, we all need to eat fat. No question. However, when we eat fat in the form of whole foods, like walnuts, sesame seeds, or flaxseeds, instead of their extracted oils, we get a beautiful, health-promoting symphony of nutrients along with the fat; that includes fiber, flavonoids, isoflavones, and other disease-fighting warriors. When you eat fat in the form of whole foods, you consume fewer calories and get a valuable supply of nutrients. Seeds contain folate, iron, calcium, niacin, lignans, and flavonoids; the oils from seeds contain almost none of these nutrients. Additionally, the fibers in the nuts and seeds bind fat and pull fat calories out of you into the toilet, so all the calories eaten are not absorbed.

COCONUT BUTTER VS. COCONUT OIL

Coconut oil has received a lot of attention in the media for its health properties, but don't be fooled by the non-scientifically validated hype. Remember, all oils, including coconut oil are very high in calories and contain insignificant nutrients. Coconut butter is different. Coconut oil is processed and is only the fat of the natural coconut. In contrast, coconut butter retains much of the fiber, vitamins, minerals and micronutrients present in the original whole coconut.

The consistency of coconut butter is similar to most other nut butters in that it is thick, creamy and rich. Where it differs is when it is chilled. When stored in the refrigerator, it hardens completely. I recommend storing it in the cabinet. It's perfect for making raw, no-bake desserts and fillings harden without having to resort to oils. You can make your own coconut butter by processing shredded coconut in a food processor until you have a smooth butter or you can purchase coconut butter online or in most health food stores.

There is a very good reason why you will not find white flour in any of the recipes within this book. Refined carbohydrates like white flour are missing the fiber and nutrients from the original grain, so they raise blood glucose higher and faster than their intact, unprocessed counterparts. The glycemic load (GL) of white bread is 75 compared to 51 for whole-wheat bread (this is on a scale of 0-100). Foods low on the glycemic index (GI) scale tend to release glucose slowly and steadily. Foods high on the glycemic index release glucose rapidly. The slow and steady release of glucose in low-glycemic foods is helpful in keeping blood glucose under control.

White flour enters the bloodstream as simple sugar and just like other forms of sugar it promotes unhealthy weight gain and increases your risk of developing heart disease. In an eight-year Italian study that followed the glycemic load of the diets of women, the women with the highest intake of high-glycemic foods were more than twice as likely to develop heart disease, an increased risk of 124 percent.[13] In another six-year study of 65,000 women, those with diets high in refined carbohydrates from white bread, white rice, and pasta were 2.5 times as likely to be diagnosed with type 2 diabetes compared to those who ate lower-GL foods such as intact whole grains and whole-wheat bread.[14] White bread also leads to an increased risk of cancer.[15]

A study involving over 500 women at Tufts University examined the diets of each participant, determining which type of food was the most prominent in each woman's daily caloric intake: healthy food, white bread, alcohol, sweets, or meat and potatoes. Astonishingly, the diet style which produced the largest increase in the size of the participants' waist measurements was white bread.[16] Shocking!

Combining nutrient-void, high-glycemic sweeteners in dessert recipes along with white flour is essentially a recipe for later-life disease disaster. I often see delicious looking "healthy" recipes include a combination of ingredients such as "coconut oil, coconut sugar, maple syrup and flour," which are actually the perfect combination of ingredients to give a person serious health problems later in life and a premature death.

White bread is white because it's been chemically bleached, just like you bleach your clothes. This means that when you eat white bread, you are also eating residual chemical bleach. Flour mills use different chemical bleaches, like oxides of nitrogen and chlorine and benzoyl peroxide mixed with chemical salts. Use of chlorine and peroxides is not allowed in the European Union.

When the wheat germ and bran are removed from the grain and only the endosperm is left (which occurs in the making of white flour products), all vitamin E and roughly 50 percent of calcium, 70 percent of phosphorus, 80 percent of iron, 98 percent of magnesium, 75 percent of manganese, 80 percent of thiamin, 75 percent of niacin, and countless more nutrients are lost. When we eat such low-nutrient foods, we are torturing our cells and robbing them of the nutrients they require to perform basic functions and to repair themselves from damage.

FLAXSEED AND CHIA SEED "EGGS" ARE THE PERFECT EGG SUBSTITUTE IN BAKING

The majority of recipes within these pages include flax "eggs." I like to use ground flaxseeds more than ground chia seeds, but this is a personal preference. Both seeds, when ground up and mixed with the right amount of liquid, form a gel-like consistency, which resembles the consistency of eggs. In the world of vegan baking, flax "eggs" and chia "eggs" are ideal egg substitutes. Either water or non-dairy milk can be mixed with the ground seeds.

To make one flax or chia "egg," mix 1 tablespoon of ground flaxseeds or chia seeds with 3 tablespoons water or non-dairy milk. To make two "eggs," mix 2 heaping tablespoons with ½ cup non-dairy milk or water. Most of my recipes use two "eggs." You will want to stir the ground flaxseeds or chia seeds with the liquid in a cup or small bowl and let sit for at least five minutes before using. These "eggs" work wonderfully for breads, muffins, brownies, cookies, cakes and more.

GROUND VANILLA VS. VANILLA EXTRACT

If there is anything I have learned of substance about nutrition, it is unequivocal that the whole food contains more substance, aka nutrients, than any refined or processed version. In the culinary arts, the whole food generally contains more flavor as well. This is no different for vanilla! Ground vanilla bean is superior to vanilla extract both in terms of nutritional value and taste. If you've ever had a dish or treat made with raw vanilla bean powder versus an extract, you know there's nothing out there like the real thing. The beans are sun-dried and cured which produces their flavor, then sold either in whole bean form, pre-scraped or powdered form, vanilla bean paste (often with added sugars which should be avoided) or soaked with alcohol or alcohol-free alternatives (like glycerin) to produce an extract or food flavoring. Because vanilla extract is processed and diluted, it cannot be counted on for ground vanilla's micronutrients including unique phytonutrients and antioxidants.

Words for the wise: Watch out for fake vanilla! Vanillin is what you'll find on labels of cheap extracts at your grocery store, also labeled "imitation vanilla." Imitation vanilla may also be called "vanilla flavor," and it's frequently combined with sugar, corn syrup or a similar unhealthful, low-quality sweetener to make products taste better. Imitation vanilla is chemically produced in laboratories to mimic the taste of vanilla but is not actually, true vanilla. Real vanilla does cost a few extra dollars, but can be purchased affordably online. Also note, real vanilla has a deep, almost smoky, rich flavor that fake vanilla cannot replace. When purchasing vanilla bean powder, make sure that the origin is stated on the label and the only ingredients are ground vanilla beans, not sugar and other flavorings too.

SHARING AND ENJOYING RECIPES WITH FRIENDS AND FAMILY

Most of the recipes within these pages make serving sizes large enough to share with friends and/or family. It's fun to see what people's reactions are when they aren't aware that what they are eating is actually good for them. Introducing the idea of healthy desserts to someone both interested in their own health and yours can inspire a person you care about to follow in your footsteps and support you in your efforts to be healthy. While the desserts inside these pages are pleasurable, they are even more pleasurable when you have friends and family to share them with. Maintaining positive habits is always easier and more enjoyable when the people in your life support and encourage you and vice versa.

Some of the recipes in this book accompany a poem as my imagination in creating these recipes instinctually made me want to create poems simultaneously and I had so much fun baking and writing together.

Imaginations are powerful things. As Albert Einstein said, "Logic will get you from A to B, but imagination will take you anywhere." My imagination says, "Delicious desserts call for delicious thoughts that make you feel inspired as you work."

Now that the science is behind us, it's time for deliciously creative fun in your kitchen. If you don't think you have a knack for baking or preparing desserts, try a few of the recipes and I am sure that will change forever. I hope you have as much pleasure making the recipes as I did.

Head to my website, Facebook and Instagram pages for an online community of like-minded health enthusiasts and health food foodies.

Website: www.taliafuhrman.com
To view the scientific references, visit: www.taliafuhrman.com/dessertstolivefor/references
Facebook: www.facebook.com/taliafuhrman
Instagram: @taliafuhrman & @taliastreats

HOW LONG WILL THESE RECIPES LAST?

Most of the recipes within these pages will last about a week if stored in the refrigerator and a couple of months if stored in the freezer. I love to cut breads and brownies into reasonable servings and freeze them, so I have a delicious treat ready for me to heat up and enjoy every day of the week. Usually a minute of warming in the microwave will do the trick.

Cookies

&

CHAPTER 1

Plant foods possess two types of magic. There is magic in the unique symphony of thousands upon thousands of nutrients, but there is also magic in the sensuous creativity of well-practiced culinary arts.

Truffles

Before I fell
in love with words
in sunsets over rolling hills
and in the winds graceful blowing daffodils.
I discovered that the truest beauty of all,
was in my perception of everything I saw
and my ability to never let a day pass by
without appreciating all of the reasons why.
For it was my own body and mind so shrewd
to thank for saturating me with ever-present gratitude
in a world in which I could have taken on any attitude.
Given that our home planet is filled with both gloom and light,
it is an exquisite experience to find that my mind is right
for choosing so much simplistic thrill
from each morning to every night.

LADYFINGER COOKIES

MAKES
26 COOKIES

PREHEAT
350°F

PREP TIME
15 MINUTES

COOK TIME
20 MINUTES

Wet Ingredients

13 medjool dates, pitted

⅓ cup non-dairy milk (use your favorite)

2 tablespoons lemon juice (optional)

½ very ripe, large banana or 1 small banana

¾ cup raw cashews, soaked overnight or ½ cup raw cashew butter

Dry Ingredients

2 tablespoons ground flaxseeds

1 teaspoon baking powder

1 teaspoon vanilla bean powder

2 cups buckwheat, spelt or oat flour (or a mix of them)

Preheat oven to 350 degrees F.

Whisk dry ingredients into a medium-sized bowl. Process all wet ingredients in food processor until combined. You may need to turn off the processor and mix with a large spoon and restart. If too thick in some areas, add a few tablespoons of water. Pour processed wet ingredients into bowl containing dry ingredients, and mix well.

With spoon, mold one rounded teaspoon of batter into Ladyfinger shape and place on a cookie sheet. A silicone pad or parchment paper works well, as they don't stick and you don't have to use oil. Bake for 20 minutes until slightly golden. Once the cookies have completely cooled, enjoy them as is or use them to make tiramisu (recipe on page 132). They will last up to five days stored in the fridge and for months stored in the freezer.

Ladyfingers date back to the House of Savoy in eleventh century France when they were enjoyed as delicate sponge cakes by the wealthy. The traditional recipe has changed little in nine hundred years and was carried throughout Europe by the marriages of the numerous daughters of Bertha of Savoy to the scattered thrones of Europe.

Flash forward to today and Ladyfingers are viewed as a delicacy and, by many, to be one of the rarest of the bakers' arts. The name Ladyfingers is self-explanatory as they are cakes roughly shaped like fingers. You can shape these cookies into the traditional shape of ladyfingers, which is to make them look like a lady's "fingers" or bars.

UNCLASSIC CHOCOLATE COOKIES

MAKES
14 COOKIES

PREHEAT
350°F

PREP TIME
12 MINUTES

COOK TIME
30 MINUTES

2 large, ripe bananas

10 medjool dates, pitted

2 flax "eggs"
(2 tablespoons ground flaxseeds + ½ cup non-dairy milk of choice)

2 tablespoons maca powder

1 teaspoon baking powder

1 teaspoon baking soda

1 teaspoon ceylon cinnamon

½ cup cocoa powder

½ cup almond flour

2¼ cups oat flour

½ cup dark chocolate chips or peanut butter chips (optional)

Preheat oven to 350 degrees F.

Prepare flax "eggs" by mixing the ground flaxseeds with ½ cup of your favorite non-dairy milk. Stir the flaxseeds with the liquid and let sit for a few minutes to form a gel.

Add bananas, pitted dates, flax "eggs," maca powder, baking powder, baking soda and cinnamon to a food processor and process these ingredients. Then add cocoa powder and process that in. Add almond flour next and process in well. Lastly, process in the oat flour in ½ cup increments.

Once processed into a dough, pour dough into a bowl, cover and refrigerate for at least one hour so that the dough is firm enough to form balls. Press down on balls with the palm of cleaned hands to form cookies.

Place batter into 8x8 inch baking pan lined with parchment paper. Top and/or mix with chocolate morsels and press lightly into batter. Bake for 30 minutes. Once removed from oven, lift out of baking pan and cool on a rack.

MACA CHOCOLATE CHIP COOKIES

MAKES
14 COOKIES

PREHEAT
350°F

PREP TIME
12 MINUTES

COOK TIME
15-18 MINUTES

2 flax "eggs"
   (2 tablespoons
   ground flaxseeds + ½ cup
   of non-dairy milk)

13 medjool dates, pitted

½ cup cooked or canned white
   beans

2 teaspoons baking powder

2 tablespoons raw cashew
   butter

1 tablespoon maca powder

1 teaspoon cinnamon

½ teaspoon nutmeg

2 cups oat flour

¾ cup 85% dark chocolate
   morsels

Preheat oven to 350 degrees F.

Prepare flax "eggs" by mixing the ground flaxseeds with ½ cup of your favorite non-dairy milk. Stir the flaxseeds with the liquid and let sit for a few minutes to form a gel.

Grind whole oats or steel cut oats in a food processor to make your own oat flour or use pre-made oat flour.

Place oat flour in a bowl and put aside. In your cleaned food processor, process all other ingredients, except for chocolate chips, until smooth. Then add oat flour and process that in until you have a crumbly but soft dough. Scoop the dough out into a large bowl and gently knead in the chocolate chips.

Line a baking tray with parchment paper. Roll about 1 tablespoon of dough into a ball. Place on the tray and using your palm, press the dough until it forms a flat cookie. You can make the cookies thick or thin, but remember that they will require less baking time the thinner you make them.

Bake for 15-18 minutes and let cool completely, at least fifteen minutes, to allow them to get crispy.

PEANUT BUTTER BLISS COOKIES

MAKES
15 COOKIES

PREHEAT
350°F

PREP TIME
12 MINUTES

COOK TIME
15-20 MINUTES

2 flax "eggs"
(2 tablespoons ground
flaxseeds + ½ cup
non-dairy milk)

1 teaspoon baking powder

½ teaspoon baking soda

1 teaspoon vanilla bean powder

12 medjool dates, pitted

¾ cup peanut butter

½ cup almond flour

½ cup oat flour

½ cup 85% dark chocolate chips

Preheat oven to 350 degrees F.

Prepare flax "eggs" by mixing the ground flaxseeds with ½ cup of your favorite non-dairy milk. Stir the flaxseeds with the liquid and let sit for a few minutes to form a gel.

Place all ingredients except oat flour (including flaxseed "eggs") in a food processor and process until smooth.

Once completely processed, pour in oat flour. Process until you have a crumbly but soft dough.

Line pan with parchment paper. Roll about 1 heaping tablespoon of dough into a ball. Place on the pan and using your palm, press until the dough forms a flat cookie.

Bake for 15-20 minutes and let cool completely to attain ultimate crispiness.

If saved in the freezer, heat for a minute before eating.

RASPBERRY JAM THUMBPRINT COOKIE

MAKES
15 COOKIES

PREHEAT
350°F

PREP TIME
15 MINUTES

COOK TIME
15-20 MINUTES

For the raspberry jam

2 cups fresh raspberries

3 tablespoons date sugar*

2 tablespoons chia seeds

For the cookie

½ cup oat flour

1 cup almond flour

¼ cup almond butter

1 teaspoon almond extract

10 medjool dates, pitted

*Date sugar is simply ground up dates and can be purchased in many health food stores and/or online.

Preheat oven to 350 degrees F.

Begin preparing the raspberry jam by cooking raspberries in a small sauce pan on medium-high heat for 5-10 minutes. Once the berries begin to bubble, turn down the heat to medium-low and allow the raspberries cook for a few more minutes. Add the date sugar and chia seeds and cook for an additional minute. Remove from heat and allow to cool.

Using a food processor, mix all the cookie ingredients.

Roll out small balls of dough about an inch in diameter and slightly flatten them into cookie shape on a baking mat or parchment paper.

Using your thumb, press down into the center of each ball to form a good indent for the raspberry jam. Place a small spoonful of jam into the center of each cookie and bake for 15-20 minutes or until cookies are golden around the edges.

Allow to cool for at least 10 minutes.

The name, thumbprint, comes from the way the cookie is prepared; press the center down with your thumb and make a "print" for the jam filling. Thumbprint cookies have been a versatile cookie with many variations, so my variation is one that doesn't employ any of the typical noxious ingredients used to prepare them like butter, sugar, eggs, or white flour.

NUTSY CHOCOLATE CHIP COOKIES

MAKES
18 COOKIES

PREHEAT
350°F

PREP TIME
15 MINUTES

COOK TIME
15 MINUTES

2 flax "eggs"
  (2 tablespoons ground
  flaxseeds + ½ cup
  non-dairy milk)
½ cup walnut butter*
13 medjool dates, pitted
1 very ripe large banana
½ cup garbanzo beans
2 tablespoons raw cashew butter
1 teaspoon vanilla bean powder
2 teaspoons baking powder
½ cup almond flour**
¾ cup oat flour
¾ cup whole-wheat flour
½ cup 85% dark chocolate chips
organic raisins or dried cherries
  to mix in and/or for topping
  (optional)

*Walnut butter is simply blended
raw walnuts that first convert
into a moist powder and then
are blended further to become
a butter.

**Almond flour is just ground-up
raw almonds.

Preheat oven to 350 degrees F.

Prepare flax "eggs" by mixing the ground flaxseeds with ½ cup of your favorite non-dairy milk. Stir the flaxseeds with the liquid and let sit for a few minutes to form a gel.

Add the flax "eggs" to a food processor along with the walnut butter, medjool dates, banana, garbanzo beans, cashew butter, vanilla and baking powder. Process for a minute or so until all ingredients are completely combined.

Add almond flour, oat flour and whole-wheat flour and process again for about 30 seconds until flours are incorporated into the batter. Pour the processed dough into a large mixing bowl.

Stir in dark chocolate chips (and raisins or dried cherries, if desired.) With your hands, roll about 1 heaping tablespoon of dough into a ball. Flatten the ball and place on a baking sheet. Top each cookie with a bit of chocolate chips and bake for about 15 minutes or until you can poke a fork or toothpick in the top and it comes out clean.

LEMON COOKIES

MAKES
16 COOKIES

PREHEAT
350°F

PREP TIME
20 MINUTES

COOK TIME
12-15 MINUTES

3 flax "eggs"
(3 tablespoon ground
flaxseeds + ¾ cup
non-dairy milk)

1 teaspoon vanilla bean powder

¼ cup raw cashew butter

14 medjool dates, pitted

1 lemon

1 ½ teaspoon lemon extract

¼ teaspoon nutmeg

½ teaspoon baking soda

¾ cup almond flour

1 ¼ cup oat flour

Preheat oven to 350 degrees F.

Place silpat (silicone mat) or parchment paper on a cookie sheet.

Prepare flax "eggs" by mixing the ground flaxseeds with ¾ cup of your favorite non-dairy milk. Stir the flaxseeds with the liquid and let sit for a few minutes to form a gel.

Zest the lemon. Squeeze out the juice from the lemon into a cup. Make sure you do not grate any of the white part of the lemon, as that is bitter.

If your pitted dates are hard, soften them by putting them in warm water for 5 minutes.

Pour the flax "eggs" into a food processor along with the vanilla, cashew butter, pitted dates, nutmeg, lemon juice and lemon zest. Process for a minute or so until all ingredients are combined and creamy. In a medium bowl, add the almond flour, oat flour and baking soda and whisk until all combined. Then take the processed "wet mixture" and add to the flour bowl and mix until blended.

Scoop with spoon, roll into balls, place on baking sheet and press down to flatten.

Bake for 12-15 minutes (until the bottom is golden brown) and allow to cool for at least 5 minutes. They will be soft and chewy.

PUMPKIN SPICE COOKIES

MAKES
14 COOKIES

PREHEAT
350°F

PREP TIME
15 MINUTES

COOK TIME
20 MINUTES

2 flax "eggs"
(2 heaping tablespoons ground flaxseeds + ½ cup non-dairy milk)

1 (15 oz.) can pumpkin

15 medjool dates, pitted, softened

2 teaspoons cinnamon

1 teaspoon nutmeg

1 teaspoon pumpkin pie spice

½ teaspoon turmeric

3 tablespoons raw cashew butter

1 teaspoon vanilla bean powder

2 teaspoons baking powder

2½ cups oat flour

½ cup rolled or old-fashioned oats

½ cup 85% dark chocolate chips, nibs and/or organic raisins

Preheat oven to 350 degrees F.

Prepare flax "eggs" by mixing the ground flaxseeds with ½ cup of your favorite non-dairy milk. Stir the flaxseeds with the liquid and let sit for a few minutes to form a gel.

Pit the dates and soften them by soaking them in warm water for 5 minutes. Blend the softened dates, flax "eggs," pumpkin, and all spices in a food processor. Once mixed, add raw cashew butter, vanilla and baking powder and mix well.

Pour into a mixing bowl and stir in the oat flour, oats and chocolate chips and/or raisins. Shape into cookies and place on silicone pad or parchment paper lined cookie sheet.

Bake for 20 minutes or until the cookies have slightly risen.

Turmeric nutrition facts: The spice turmeric is so healthy that a party should be thrown in its honor. If someone does throw it a party, I'd love to be invited. Turmeric has a deep history as a natural medicine with significant disease prevention capabilities. The spice is native to India and Southeast Asia, where it has been popular in cuisines for several thousand years.

Turmeric reduces the risk of, and can aid in the treatment of certain types of cancer such as cancers of the colon, pancreas, skin, mouth and vulva, as well as breast cancer. For centuries, turmeric has been employed to reduce inflammation and it may be able to improve endothelial function – the ability of our arteries to relax normally, protecting against heart attacks, strokes and dementia.[1]

In addition to its culinary use, turmeric has remained a mainstay herb in botanical medicine, with medical usage going back thousands of years in the Ayurvedic tradition.

BANANA OAT COOKIES

MAKES
15 COOKIES

PREHEAT
350°F

PREP TIME
15 MINUTES

COOK TIME
12-15 MINUTES

2 large, very ripe bananas

1 teaspoon baking powder

10 medjool dates, pitted

2 tablespoons raw almond butter

1 teaspoon cinnamon

1 teaspoon nutmeg

1 teaspoon vanilla bean powder

½ cup almond flour*

1 cup oat flour*

1 cup rolled or old-fashioned oats

½ cup organic raisins

1 tablespoon shredded coconut

1 tablespoon hemp seeds or pumpkin seeds

*Almond "flour" is simply ground up almonds, and oat "flour" is simply ground up oats.

Preheat oven to 350 degrees F.

Add the bananas to a food processor along with the baking powder, pitted dates, raw almond butter, cinnamon, nutmeg and vanilla. Process for a minute then add the almond and oat flour and process for another minute.

Pour the cookie dough into a large bowl and stir in the raisins, shredded coconut and pumpkin seeds.

Place dough in the fridge to get firm for 15 minutes.

With wet hands, scoop 1 heaping tablespoon of the mixture and form a ball, then flatten onto a lined baking tray. You should have enough to make 14 to 16 cookies.

Bake for 12-15 minutes or until slightly golden on the outside.

33

GREEN TEA COOKIES

MAKES
22 COOKIES

PREHEAT
350ºF

PREP TIME
15 MINUTES

COOK TIME
15 MINUTES

---

2 flax "eggs"
(2 tablespoons ground
flaxseeds + ½ cup
non-dairy milk)

½ cup raw cashew butter

15 medjool dates, pitted

2 teaspoons baking powder

1 tablespoon green tea powder

1 tablespoon maca powder

1 teaspoon vanilla bean powder

1½ cups oat flour

¾ cup organic raisins and/or
85% dark chocolate chips

2 tablespoons shredded coconut

Preheat oven to 350 degrees F.

Prepare flax "eggs" by mixing the ground flaxseeds with ½ cup of your favorite non-dairy milk. Stir the flaxseeds with the liquid and let sit for a few minutes to form a gel.

Pour the flax "eggs" into a food processor along with the raw cashew butter, dates, baking powder, green tea powder, maca powder and vanilla. Process for a minute or so until all ingredients are combined. Add the oat flour to the food processor and process for a few minutes until a dough is formed.

Pour the dough into a large mixing bowl. Stir in the raisins and shredded coconut.

Scoop out a few tablespoons of dough onto a baking tray until you finish using all of the batter. Flatten the dough with your hands to make them into cookie shapes.

Bake for 15 minutes or until lightly golden on top. Don't overbake. Cookie should be crunchy outside and soft inside; they will continue to cook and harden once removed from the oven.

Polyphenols, like flavonoids and catechins, are abundant in green tea. These powerful antioxidants reduce the formation of free radicals in the body, protecting cells and molecules from damage; hence green tea is an anti-aging food. One of the more powerful compounds in green tea is the antioxidant Epigallocatechin Gallate (EGCG), which has been studied to prevent cancer.[2]

Maca has been cultivated as a vegetable crop in Peru for at least 3000 years. Maca is a relative of the radish and has an odor and taste similar to butterscotch. Maca's high-nutrient and plant proteins help keep our bones and teeth healthy, promotes wound healing and vitality.

Flaxseeds are lignan warriors, containing many times the amount of lignans, or natural cancer-protective compounds, of any other food. Flax, chia, and hemp seeds are also very rich in omega-3 fatty acids and have substantial anti-inflammatory properties.[3]

SWEET POTATO SPICE COOKIES

MAKES
15 COOKIES

PREHEAT
300°F

PREP TIME*
30 MINUTES

COOK TIME
12-15 MINUTES

1 cup oat flour

1 cup almond flour

1 teaspoon baking powder

1 teaspoon baking soda

1 teaspoon ground cinnamon

½ teaspoon vanilla bean powder

½ teaspoon cream of tartar

½ teaspoon cardamon

¼ teaspoon ginger

1 cup sweet potato puree** (can substitute with pumpkin puree)

¼ cup almond butter

6 pitted medjool dates (soften in warm water for 5 minutes, then drain to use)

⅓ cup whipped aquafaba

optional: currants

**To bake sweet potato, wrap in foil, and bake at 400°F for 45 minutes, until the sweet potato is tender enough to poke with a fork, then blend to make the puree

Preheat oven to 300 degrees F.

Sift all dry ingredients in medium bowl (first nine ingredients). Set aside.

In a blender, add sweet potato, almond butter and medjool dates and blend until well blended. Add dry ingredients and mix completely.

Strain a can of chick peas, with the liquid (aquafaba) being strained into its own bowl. Whip the aquafaba until it's thick; this can take as long as 10 minutes. Fold into cookie mixture.

Using a teaspoon, scoop onto cookie sheets. Bake for 12-15 minutes. Remove from cookie sheet and place on cooling rack.

Store them in the refrigerator. I like them when they are not so cold, so I take out a couple of cookies and let them sit for about a half hour before I eat them with my tea.

*Assumes sweet potato is already cooked

Aquafaba is the liquid portion in a can of chickpeas. Its chemical composition allows it to be whipped up, but it can take some time, so don't get discouraged. You can whip it up with an electric mixer or with a hand mixer, but it will take longer with a hand mixer. You can add some cream of tartar (just a pinch) to make the whipping happen more easily.

SPICED WALNUT COOKIES

MAKES
10 COOKIES

PREHEAT
350ºF

PREP TIME
15 MINUTES

COOK TIME
15 MINUTES

2 flax "eggs"
   (2 tablespoons ground
   flaxseeds + ½ cup water or
   non-dairy milk)

12 medjool dates, pitted

1 teaspoon baking powder

1 teaspoon cinnamon

1 teaspoon ginger

¼ teaspoon nutmeg

¼ teaspoon ground cloves

A pinch of spicy smoked paprika

¼ cup coconut butter

¼ cup walnut butter (can use
   sesame seed butter aka tahini
   or cashew butter instead)

1 cup oat flour

¼ cup non-dairy milk

½ cup 85% dark chocolate
   chips, organic raisins or dried
   cherries (optional, I have made
   them with and without and love
   them both ways)

Preheat oven to 350 degrees F.

Prepare flax "eggs" by mixing 2 heaping tablespoons ground flaxseeds with ½ cup water or non-dairy milk. Stir and let sit for a minute.

Pit dates before you add them to the food processor along with the flax "eggs," baking powder, all spices, and both butters. Process until all ingredients are thoroughly combined. Add the oat flour to the food processor and process for another minute or so until the oat flour is fully incorporated.

Pour this mixture into a large mixing bowl and stir in non-dairy milk (this helps the dough bind together) and dark chocolate chips, if using.

Line a baking tray with parchment paper or tinfoil.

Take about 2-3 tablespoons of dough and shape cookies so they're round and then flatten them with your hands. Place each one on the baking pan and repeat this process until there is no dough left.

Bake for 15 minutes or until just golden. They will be soft when you take them out of the oven, but they will harden as they cool.

40

STRAWBERRY SHORTCAKE COOKIES

MAKES
14 COOKIES

PREHEAT
350°F

PREP TIME
15 MINUTES

COOK TIME
40 MINUTES

2 flax "eggs"
(2 heaping tablespoons
ground flaxseeds + ½ cup
non-dairy milk of choice)

1 large apple of choice, cut into
chunks and core removed

10 medjool dates, pitted

2 teaspoons ground vanilla bean
powder

2 teaspoons baking powder

2 heaping tablespoons coconut
butter (can sub cashew or
almond butter)*

1 cup almond flour

2 cups oat flour

1 cup organic strawberries, tops
removed and sliced

*Any of these butters will work
beautifully, I've tried all three.

Preheat oven to 350 degrees F.

Mix ground flaxseeds with non-dairy milk and let set for a minute to create flax "eggs."

Cut up apple into chunks. You don't have to peel it if it is organic. If it is not organic, I recommend peeling. Place the apple chunks in your food processor. Process thoroughly. Add flax "eggs" to food processor with pitted medjool dates, vanilla bean and baking powder. Process again until the mixture is well combined. If using coconut butter, it may be hardened and need softening. Heat in the microwave for 30 seconds if it is hard. Add softened coconut butter (or nut butter) to the food processor. Process with the rest of the mixture.

Add almond flour to the mixture. Process well. Lastly add oat flour and process until a nice, evenly mixed batter forms. This shouldn't take more than a few minutes.

Wash and slice up strawberries. Mix them into the batter to your liking. Mold into cookies and place them on a parchment-lined baking tray. Top with additional strawberry slices if desired. Bake for 40 minutes or until they are nice and golden on top.

Research indicates a large benefit of consuming strawberries is that doing so helps the aging brain maintain peak mental performance in later years. Most people think of blueberries as the best food for promoting brain health and mental clarity, yet strawberries are just as worthy as blueberries. In fact, strawberries have more micronutrients per calorie. With only 49 calories per cup, strawberries are extremely low in calories and packed with one heck of a nutrient punch.

Strawberries get their powerful nutrient punch from vitamin C, calcium, magnesium and potassium and they are a rich source of phenolic antioxidants and flavonoids. Phenolic antioxidants are a group of antioxidants that improve our health by promoting weight loss, reducing disease risk, reversing inflammation and reducing pain.[4] How impressive is that?

FLOURLESS ALMOND GINGER COOKIES

MAKES
17 COOKIES

PREHEAT
350°F

PREP TIME
30 MINUTES

COOK TIME
10-12 MINUTES

1 teaspoon ground ginger

½ teaspoon cinnamon

½ teaspoon nutmeg

½ teaspoon ground cloves

½ cup almond butter

½ cup non-dairy milk of choice

2 teaspoons baking powder

14 medjool dates, pitted

½ cup almond flour*

*You can purchase almond flour or make your own. Simply grind up raw almonds in a high-powdered blender or food processor until a fine powder forms. Don't blend too long – too much blending will churn the powder into butter.

Preheat oven to 350 degrees F.

In a food processor, combine ginger, cinnamon, nutmeg, cloves, almond butter, non-dairy milk, baking powder and dates. Process until all ingredients have been thoroughly mixed.

Add almond flour and process again for a minute or so until a smooth dough is formed. The dough will be a bit dense, but this is okay.

Pour the cookie dough in a large mixing bowl. If you desire perfectly shaped cookies, freeze the moist dough for 20 minutes before shaping into balls and flattening into cookies. Alternatively, you can simply use the dough straight from the food processor.

Using a large spoon or your hands, scoop up about three tablespoons of batter and roll it into a ball. Flatten the ball to create a cookie and place on a baking sheet. Repeat this step until all of the cookies are formed.

If desired, decorate the tops of each one by using a large fork and pressing the fork down in the middle of each cookie and then again perpendicularly (see photo). Bake for 10-12 minutes.

Cool for about 10 minutes and they will be ready for eating. Do not overbake. The final cookies should be a bit fluffy rather than hard. Overbaking will result in hard cookies. The cookies will harden overnight.

These are entirely flourless, for almond "flour" is simply ground-up almonds. These cookies are great when warmed in the oven. Of course, we need our veggies and fresh fruit, but scrumptious cookies that contribute to good health can certainly be a part of what makes us shine brightly.

ICE CREAM SCOOP COOKIES

MAKES
10 COOKIES

PREHEAT
350ºF

PREP TIME
10 MINUTES

COOK TIME
15-20 MINUTES

½ cup water or non-dairy milk

10 medjool dates, pitted

1 cup cooked or canned white beans

1 teaspoon vanilla bean powder

1 ½ teaspoon baking powder

½ cup oat flour

½ cup almond flour

¼ cup smooth peanut butter or coconut butter

1 cup whole-wheat flour

¼ cup dark chocolate chips (or organic raisins)

¼ cup unsweetened shredded coconut

Preheat oven to 350 degrees F.

Mix all flours in a large bowl and set mixture aside. Blend all other ingredients (except chocolate chips) in a high-powered blender or food processor until evenly mixed.

Using a large spoon or spatula, pour the wet mixture out of the blender and into the large bowl with the dry ingredients and mix well. Now add the chocolate chips (or raisins).

Using an ice cream scoop, scoop out a few tablespoons of batter, getting about 9 to 12 cookies and place on parchment paper or silicone baking sheet. Bake for about 15-20 minutes or until the cookies are crisp/hard on top.

PECAN RAISIN COOKIES

MAKES
9 COOKIES

PREHEAT
300°F

PREP TIME*
15 MINUTES

COOK TIME
15 MINUTES

½ cup sweet potato, peeled and cooked*

1 (15 oz.) white beans or garbanzo beans, cooked, canned works

12 medjool dates, pitted

2 tablespoons peanut butter

1 teaspoon cinnamon

1 teaspoon nutmeg

1 teaspoon vanilla bean powder

1 teaspoon baking powder

1 ½ cup oat flour or spelt flour (or half and half combo)

1 tablespoon maca powder

⅓ cup rolled or old-fashioned oats

½ cup raw pecans, chopped (optional)

⅓ cup organic raisins

⅓ cup dark chocolate chips or carob chips (optional)

*To bake sweet potato, wrap in foil, and bake at 400°F for 45 minutes, until the sweet potato is tender enough to poke with a fork

Preheat oven to 300 degrees F.

To make cookies, process all ingredients (except for oat or spelt flour, oats, pecans, raisins, and chocolate chips) in a food processor until smooth. Add oat (or spelt) flour to the food processor and process that into the batter well.

Pour into a large mixing bowl and mix in the oats, pecans, raisins and chocolate chips. Voila! It's almost done.

Scoop individual tablespoons of the mixture onto a parchment paper lined baking tray or silicone baking sheet until the batter is completely used. Slightly flatten each one with your clean hands.

Bake for 15 minutes or until lightly brown. Make sure not to overcook if you desire a crunchy outside and soft inside. They will continue to cook and harden once you remove them from the oven. Let sit for at least 15 minutes before enjoying.

*Assumes sweet potato is already cooked.

PEANUT BUTTER ESPRESSO TRUFFLES

MAKES
9 TRUFFLES

METHOD
REFRIGERATE

PREP TIME
20 MINUTES

CHILL TIME
1 HOUR

10 medjool dates, pitted
¼ cup smooth peanut butter
5 tablespoons cocoa powder
1½ teaspoons ground coffee
1 teaspoon vanilla bean powder
⅓ cup 85% dark chocolate chips

Optional toppings:
freeze-dried raspberries
unsweetened shredded coconut
cacao powder

In a food processor, process dates, peanut butter, cocoa powder, ground coffee and vanilla bean powder. Process until smooth and creamy.

Heat dark chocolate chips in the microwave for one minute, stir and add to the food processor. Process until you achieve a smooth and creamy mixture.

Pour mixture into a mixing bowl and with your hands, mold into truffle balls. I used about 1 heaping tablespoon to create each truffle. Roll truffles in optional toppings, if desired.

Once rolled in optional toppings, chill for at least 1 hour in the refrigerator before serving.

MATCHA CASHEW TRUFFLES

MAKES
8 TRUFFLES

METHOD
REFRIGERATE

PREP TIME
20 MINUTES

CHILL TIME
3 HOURS

8 medjool dates, pitted
¼ cup almond flour
1 teaspoon vanilla bean powder
3 tablespoons hemp seeds
1 teaspoon matcha powder
¼ cup cashew butter
coconut shreds, to roll them in

Soften dates if necessary by putting them in warm water for 5 minutes.

Add the dates to your food processor along with the rest of the ingredients except for the shredded coconut. Process until smooth and evenly mixed.

Once mixed in the food processor, roll them in coconut shreds to a size to your liking. I used about 1 heaping tablespoon of mixture to create each truffle. Refrigerate for at least 3 hours before serving.

Matcha is finely ground powder of specially grown and processed green tea. The history of matcha tea goes back all the way to the Tang Dynasty China (618-907), in which tea leaves were steamed and formed into tea bricks for storage and trade. Today, green tea matcha is a tasty, fun, colorful and even playful addition to these cashew butter-date based truffles.

Brownies

CHAPTER 2

In the process of eating more nutritiously and getting healthier, keep in mind that there are domino effects. A healthy diet can lead to more happiness, a sharper mind, more motivation and so much more. I like to think a healthy lifestyle is a foundation to a full life, one in which you aren't afraid to be silly, fail, or try something new.

"Life is like a movie, write your own ending, keep believing, keep pretending."
~Jim Henson

Blondies & Bars

Even if I am the only one that truly knows,
the extent of the journeys my crazy mind goes.
I will deem all well at the end of the day,
no matter what my logical mind will say.

It is one phenomenal truth to hold forever in your heart
for being playfully ridiculous is always very smart.

PEANUT BUTTER
BLACK BEAN BROWNIES

MAKES
8 BROWNIES

PREHEAT
350°F

PREP TIME
15 MINUTES

COOK TIME
25 MINUTES

1 cup cacao powder of choice

1 (15 oz) can black beans, aim for a BPA-free brand

12 soft medjool dates, pitted

½ cup oat flour

1 teaspoon baking powder

1 teaspoon baking soda

⅓ cup natural peanut butter (can replace with cashew or almond butter, if desired)

¼ cup water

1 teaspoon ceylon cinnamon

1 tablespoon French roast coffee or coffee of choice (optional)

85% dark chocolate chips for topping (optional)

Preheat oven to 350 degrees F.

In a food processor, add the dates, cacao powder, beans and water. Process those ingredients completely and then added all other ingredients (except chocolate chip topping). Process thoroughly.

Use a glass baking dish (8x8 inch) and place parchment paper down. Add the brownie mixture and press down with your palms to spread the mixture evenly.

Bake for 20-25 minutes. Cut brownies into squares, enjoy them as is or with your favorite non-dairy ice cream. Both ways are absolutely delicious.

TRIPLE LAYER BARS

MAKES
16 BARS

METHOD
FREEZE FOR 3 HOURS

PREP TIME
30 MINUTES

COOK TIME
NONE

For the base layer

½ cup raw cashew butter

¼ raw almond butter

10 medjool dates, pitted

1 teaspoon ground cinnamon

½ teaspoon ground nutmeg

1 ½ teaspoons vanilla bean
  powder

1 cup oat flour

½ cup almond flour

For the coconut middle layer

8 medjool dates, pitted

3 tablespoons shredded coconut

1 very ripe, medium-sized
  banana

¼ cup almond milk

1 teaspoon vanilla bean powder

For the chocolate topping

1 medium-sized ripe banana

⅓ cup cocoa powder

2 tablespoons raw cashew butter

5 medjool dates, pitted

Line an 8x8 inch pan with parchment paper or tin foil, allowing the paper or foil to hang over the edges.

To prepare the base layer, add all base layer ingredients, except the almond flour and oat flour, to a food processor and process thoroughly. Add both flours to the food processor once the other ingredients have been thoroughly combined. Process for another minute or so until both flours have been fully incorporated and a smooth dough is formed.

Press and spread the dough out evenly into your prepared pan. Flatten the top. The dough will be thin which is what you are aiming for. Freeze it while you prepare the middle coconut layer.

To prepare the middle layer, combine all ingredients in cleaned food processor. Once mixed, pour the coconut layer on top of the base layer, smoothing the top of the middle layer evenly with a large spoon, spatula or even your hands. Place in the freezer to chill while you prepare the top chocolate layer.

To prepare the top chocolate layer, combine all ingredients in cleaned food processor, and process until mixed.

Take the pan out of the freezer and pour the chocolate layer on top of the middle layer, smoothing the top. Refrigerate overnight or freeze for at least two hours until the bars are solid. Cut into bars, and store them in the freezer. Thaw one and enjoy whenever you need a treat.

Ayurveda is an ancient Indian tradition of medicine that probably originated about 600 B.C. and became known for its many herbal medicines for chronic diseases. Soon after the introduction of cashew nuts to India by the Portuguese in the sixteenth century, cashews became a favorite food and healing agent of ayurvedic medicine. Cashew nuts are still considered in India to be a good stimulant, an appetizer, a rejuvenator, a hair tonic, an aphrodisiac, and a restorative of lost vigor and sexual health.

ALMOND MOCHA BARS

MAKES
15 BARS

METHOD
FREEZE

PREP TIME
15-20 MINUTES

COOK TIME
NONE

For the almond-lemon crust

½ cup old-fashioned or rolled oats

⅓ cup mixture of almond & walnut flour

2 flax "eggs" (2 tablespoons ground flaxseeds + ½ cup non-dairy milk)

8 medjool dates, pitted

1 tablespoon lemon juice

1½ teaspoon vanilla bean powder

For the middle maca-cinnamon layer

12 medjool dates, pitted

¼ cup raw cashew butter or peanut butter

1 very ripe, large banana

1 teaspoon vanilla bean powder

1-2 tablespoons non-dairy milk

1 teaspoon cinnamon

1 tablespoon maca powder

For the espresso chocolate ganache layer

28 grams vegan dark chocolate (about 4 squares of dark unsweetened chocolate)

2 tablespoons raw cashew butter

5 medjool dates, pitted

2 tablespoons your favorite coffee granules (I used dark French roast)

2-3 tablespoons non-dairy milk

Line a square 8x8 inch pan with tin foil or parchment paper.

To prepare the crust, add all ingredients except the milk to a blender or food processor and process for about a minute until fine crumbs form.

Add the milk and process for another 30 seconds or so until the mixture begins to stick to itself. Take the mixture out of the food processor and press it down into the bottom of the pan evenly so that it is flat. Place this layer in the freezer while you prepare the middle layer.

To prepare the middle layer, again add all ingredients except the milk to a food processor and process thoroughly. This shouldn't take more than a minute.

Add the milk and scrape down the sides of the food processor, as needed. Spread this layer on top of the crust, making sure that the top is even. Place the pan back in the freezer while you prepare the top layer.

To prepare the espresso chocolate ganache, add the dates and melted chocolate (melted in the microwave for 30 seconds) to the (cleaned) food processor along with the rest of the ganache layer ingredients. Process until smooth. This shouldn't take more than a minute.

Pour the ganache in an even layer over the middle layer and place the pan in the freezer. Keep in the freezer for at least three hours before slicing and serving.

Store leftovers in the freezer.

COCONUT BLUEBERRY SQUARES

MAKES
12 BARS

PREHEAT
350°F

PREP TIME
NIGHT BEFORE
& 15 MINUTES

COOK TIME
35-40 MINUTES

---

2 flax "eggs"
(2 tablespoons ground flaxseeds + ½ cup non-dairy milk)

1 tablespoon white wine vinegar

2 teaspoons baking powder

¾ cup raw cashews soaked in water overnight and drained (or ½ cup raw cashew butter)

⅓ cup shredded coconut

1 ½ teaspoon ground vanilla bean

10 medjool dates, pitted

2 very ripe, medium-sized bananas

2½ cups whole-wheat flour or oat flour or a combo

1 cup fresh or frozen blueberries

Night before: soak cashews

Preheat oven to 350 degrees F.

Prepare the flax "eggs" by mixing the ground flaxseeds with the non-dairy milk (can also use water) and let sit for a few minutes.

Add the cashews to a food processor and process until creamy and smooth. Add the milk, vanilla, flax "eggs," pitted dates, bananas, baking powder and vinegar to the food processor and process until smooth. Add shredded coconut and flours and process again until smooth. Pour the dough into a large mixing bowl and carefully fold in the blueberries evenly.

Spread the dough out evenly in baking pan, (I used an 8x8 inch) flattening the top.

Bake for 35-40 minutes or until slightly golden on top. When you insert a toothpick or fork, it should come out clean.

Blueberries have been shown to prevent mental decline in later years and also reverse abnormal brain activity. Don't want dementia or Alzheimer's disease? Then eating more blueberries is a smart choice. They contain large amounts of tannins, an antioxidant linked to the reversal and prevention of age-related mental decline.[1]

Research shows that when an equal number of carbohydrate calories are replaced with nuts and seeds, weight loss increases. Not only do cashews have a lower fat content than most other nuts, approximately 82% of their fat is unsaturated fatty acids, plus about 66% of this unsaturated fatty acid content are heart-healthy monounsaturated fats.

CASHEW BUTTER FUDGE

MAKES
15 BARS

METHOD
FREEZE 4 HOURS

PREP TIME
20 MINUTES

COOK TIME
NONE

For the bottom chocolate layer

½ cup peanut butter or cashew butter

⅓ cup shredded coconut

1 very ripe, large banana

1 teaspoon vanilla bean powder

10 medjool dates, pitted

½ cup canned black beans

⅓ cup cocoa powder

½ cup rolled or old-fashioned oats

For the top layer

1 cup raw cashew butter

1 (15 oz) can white beans, rinsed and patted dry

10 medjool dates, pitted, softened (microwave 10-12 seconds)

1 tablespoon vanilla bean powder

½ cup pistachios, crumbled, raw and unsalted (optional)

85% dark chocolate, warmed, to use as a drizzle on top

To make the bottom chocolate layer, add peanut or cashew butter, coconut, banana, vanilla, dates and black beans to a food processor and process until smooth and creamy. Add cocoa powder and oats and process again until smooth. Pour this layer into a tinfoil-lined, square baking pan, loaf pan or muffin tin.

For the top layer, mix all ingredients except pistachios in a blender until it's a smooth mixture. Smooth the top layer onto the bottom layer. Sprinkle crumbled pistachios on top, if desired. You can also warm 85% chocolate and drizzle on top.* Place in the freezer and freeze until firm (at least 4 hours). This fudge is best stored in the freezer because it can get too soft if stored in the fridge.

*To make the chocolate drizzle, place ¼ cup 85% dark chocolate morsels in microwavable mug and microwave for 12-15 seconds. Stir. If not completely melted, microwave another 5 seconds. Drizzle over fudge as desired.

GOJI BERRY BLONDIES

MAKES
12 BLONDIES

METHOD
FREEZE

PREP TIME
20 MINUTES

COOK TIME
NONE

1 ½ cups rolled or old-fashioned oats or oat flour

1 cup walnuts

1 cup raw almonds, or 1 cup almond flour *

¾ cup dates, chopped

½ cup non-dairy milk of choice

1 large, ripe banana

1 ½ teaspoon cinnamon

1 teaspoon nutmeg

1 ½ teaspoon ground vanilla

¾ cup goji berries

½ cup shredded coconut

2 oz unsweetened dark chocolate

*Note: Almond flour is simply raw, whole almonds that have been ground into a fine powder. It can be purchased in health food stores and many supermarkets, but it is best to grind almonds and make it fresh.

In a high-powered blender, blend the oats until a flour forms (or simply use oat flour). Add to a large bowl.

Repeat process for the walnuts and almonds, being sure not to over-process them as you don't want the oils to release. Add to the bowl and gently break apart any clumps with your fingers. It's okay if a few walnut or almond pieces remain.

Add dates and non-dairy milk to food processor and process until a slurry forms. Add banana, cinnamon, nutmeg and vanilla and process until well combined. Add almond flour to the date mixture in the food processor and process until completely combined. Then add in walnut flour and do the same. Finally, add oat flour to the mixture and process until fully incorporated. With a large spoon, pour the mixture into a large mixing bowl. Once in the bowl, stir in goji berries and shredded coconut evenly.

Line an 8-inch square pan with aluminum foil or parchment paper. Scoop the dough into the pan. Dip a knife in water and spread dough until smooth. Place in the freezer for 30 minutes.

Place the unsweetened chocolate in a microwave-proof bowl and heat in the microwave for 1 minute, stir, and heat for another 30 seconds or until completely melted. Remove pan from freezer. Using a small spoon, drizzle with chocolate to add a decorative touch. Cut into squares.

Store in the freezer for a guilt-free snack. They can be eaten straight from the freezer or heated in the microwave for 30 to 45 seconds.

STRAWBERRY BLISS BROWNIES

MAKES
20 BROWNIES

PREHEAT
350°F

METHOD
REFRIGERATE

PREP TIME
NIGHT BEFORE &
20 MINUTES

For the brownie layer

4 flax "eggs"
(4 tablespoons ground
flaxseeds + 12 tablespoons
water)

½ cup oat flour

½ cup almond flour

½ cup canned black beans

½ cup cocoa powder

12 medjool dates, pitted

1 teaspoon vanilla bean powder

1 tablespoon ground coffee
(optional)

For the strawberry filling

½ cup canned coconut milk,
refrigerated overnight, then
liquid removed*

2 tablespoons coconut butter

½ cup coconut yogurt

½ cup fresh organic strawberries

1 teaspoon vanilla bean powder

1 tablespoon beetroot powder

For the coconut cream icing

½ cup canned coconut milk,
refrigerated overnight, then
liquid removed*

⅓ cup soy or coconut yogurt

5 medjool dates

1 teaspoon vanilla bean powder

*After refrigeration overnight, the
cream will have separated from
the liquid. Drain the liquid and
set aside, you will use only the
cream for this recipe.

Night before: refrigerate coconut milk

Preheat oven to 350 degrees F.

Mix flax "eggs" ingredients together. Allow to sit for 2 minutes. Add the flax "eggs" and the rest of the brownie layer ingredients to a food processor. Process until smooth and creamy. Pour the brownie ingredients into a large bowl. On a large baking sheet lined with parchment paper, smooth out and flatten the brownie layer with a large spoon and/or a cake knife. Spread out into as close to a rectangle as you can because you will be cutting this layer into squares later.

Bake the flattened brownie layer for 40-50 minutes or until it is firm and a bit crisp on top.

While the brownie layer is baking, in a clean food processor, process all of the strawberry filling ingredients. Add to another large bowl and place in the fridge for at least 15 minutes so it can firm.

Once the brownie layer is done baking, place in the refrigerator to firm up for at least two hours. Once firm, cut it in half horizontally so that you have two equal sized pieces. One will be for the top of the sandwich; the other will be for the bottom of the sandwich.

Spread a thin layer of the chilled strawberry bliss filling on each side of the halved chocolaty layers. The chocolaty layers should be firm enough that you can carefully lift one layer with your hands and stack it on top of the other layer, making sure that the strawberry filling is on the inside.

Place the large sandwich in the fridge for at least fifteen minutes and then slice into 3-4 inch squares (or whichever size you prefer).

Prepare coconut icing by processing all icing ingredients in a food processor or blending ingredients in a blender. Top squares with as much icing as you desire.

DOUBLE-DECKER FIG BROWNIES

MAKES
15 BROWNIES

PREHEAT
350°F

PREP TIME
NIGHT BEFORE
& 15 MINUTES

COOK TIME
18 MINUTES

For the brownie layer

2 flax "eggs"
(2 tablespoons ground
flaxseeds + ½ cup
non-dairy milk)

1 teaspoon baking powder

1 teaspoon baking soda

2 very ripe, medium-sized
bananas

12 medjool dates, pitted

½ cup organic dried Turkish figs
(about 6), de-stemmed and
soaked in water overnight

1 cup macadamia nuts, soaked
overnight in water (or boiled
for 5 minutes)

¾ cup cocoa powder

¾ cup oat flour

⅓ cup raw walnut pieces
(optional)

For the chocolate icing

1 ripe avocado

½ cup cocoa powder

8 medjool dates, pitted and
softened

1 teaspoons vanilla bean
powder

Optional toppings

coconut shreds

almond pieces

Note: Double the recipe for
thicker brownies or use the
above amounts for thinner treats.

Night before: soak figs, nuts

Preheat oven to 350 degrees F.

To prepare the brownie layer, first mix together the 2 flax "eggs,"
baking powder and baking soda in a small bowl or cup. Let sit for a
minute. Thoroughly drain the soaked macadamia nuts and process
in a blender or food processor until they form a fine crumble. Add
the soaked figs to the food processor along with the flaxseed mixture.
Process until you achieve a smooth, even consistency. Turn off the
food processor and add all the remaining brownie layer ingredients
except for the flour and walnut pieces. Process thoroughly. Pour the
batter into a large bowl and stir in flour with a large mixing spoon.
Mix in the walnuts. Line an 8x8 inch baking dish with parchment
paper, flatten the dough and smooth evenly. Bake for 18 minutes or
until a toothpick comes out clean.

While the brownies are baking, prepare chocolate icing. Place all
ingredients in a blender. Blend until smooth. Add a small amount
of water if needed to achieve a smooth texture. Allow baked
brownies to cool for at least 15 minutes before spreading the
chocolate icing on top. Sprinkle with coconut shreds and/or almond
pieces if desired. Let the brownies set in the fridge for 30 minutes,
cut into squares.

Like leis and pineapple, the macadamia nut is a food typically
associated with Hawaii. In fact, macadamias actually
originated from Australia. Aborigines from Down Under have
been enjoying macadamias for thousands of years. In 1857,
Scottish-Australian chemist, John Macadam, took time to
conduct research studies on the nut. It is in his honor that the
macadamia nut is named. The first macadamia tree was planted
in Hawaii in 1882. The fertile volcanic soil and warm climate
provided the ideal conditions for the trees to thrive. Today,
Hawaii is the world's largest producer of macadamia nuts.

TAHINI BROWNIES

MAKES
16 BROWNIES

PREHEAT
350°F

PREP TIME
20 MINUTES

COOK TIME
25-30 MINUTES

For the brownie layer

2 chia or flax "eggs"
  (2 tablespoons ground
  flaxseeds + ½ cup
  non-dairy milk)

2 teaspoons baking powder

1 ½ teaspoon ground vanilla
  bean

12 medjool dates, pitted

⅓ cup tahini (unhulled if
  available) or ½ cup unhulled
  sesame seeds.

1 cup cocoa powder

1 ¼ cup spelt or oat flour

For the chocolate icing

1 medium avocado

½ cup cocoa powder

6 medjool dates, softened

shredded coconut, mulberries,
  sesame seeds for garnish

Preheat oven to 350 degrees F.

Combine flax or chia "egg" ingredients. Allow "egg" to sit for 1 minute. In a food processor or blender combine all the ingredients except for the cocoa powder and flour. Process until smooth.

Add the cocoa powder and process for another minute or so until the brownie dough becomes evenly mixed. Lastly, add the flour into a large mixing bowl and with a spoon, mix in the processed dough.

Pour the dough into a parchment paper-lined 8x8 inch baking pan. Bake for 25-30 minutes or until an inserted toothpick or fork comes out clean.

While baking, prepare the chocolate icing for the top layer. Mix the avocado and cocoa powder in a blender or food processor. Once mixed, blend in the soft dates. Smooth this mixture over the baked brownies. Add shredded coconut, dried mulberry pieces or sesame seeds as garnish, if desired.

Place the brownies in the refrigerator for at least 30 minutes so that the topping can harden. Then slice and enjoy.

Tahini is nothing more than ground sesame seeds. Sesame seeds have been shown to have a cholesterol-lowering effect in humans, and supplementation with the sesame lignan sesamin reduced high blood pressure. Lignans also have anti-estrogenic effects that inhibit cell growth in breast tumors, a remarkable mechanism to improving our health and reducing disease risk.[2]

"Open sesame," the famous phrase from the Arabian Nights, reflects the distinguishing feature of the sesame seed pod, which bursts open when it reaches maturity.

CASHEW CREAM LEMON BARS

MAKES
16 BARS

PREHEAT
FREEZE

PREP TIME
NIGHT BEFORE &
20 MINUTES

COOK TIME
NONE

For the crust

¾ cup rolled or old-fashioned
  oats

½ cup almond flour

12 medjool dates, pitted

1½ teaspoon vanilla bean
  powder

**For the lemon coconut
cream filling**

2 cans full fat coconut milk
  (approximately 13 oz.),
  refrigerated overnight, then
  liquid removed*

1 cup raw cashews
  (soaked for 2 hours)

2 lemons, juiced

zest from 3 lemons

8 medjool dates, pitted

2 tablespoons non-dairy milk

1 tablespoon almond butter

1 tablespoon vanilla bean
  powder

1 tablespoon cornstarch

1 tablespoon nutritional yeast

¼ teaspoon turmeric

Shredded coconut for garnish
(optional)

*After refrigeration overnight, the
cream will have separated from
the liquid. Drain the liquid and
set aside, you will use only the
cream for this recipe.

Night before: refrigerate coconut milk

Line a 8x8 inch baking dish with parchment paper in two pieces to allow extra paper around the edges of the pan to lift the bars out later. Set aside.

Place all crust ingredients in a food processor or high-powered blender and process well. Press bottom crust layer into the baking dish, flatten and place baking dish in the freezer while you prepare the filling.

To make lemon cream filling, combine all ingredients except the coconut cream in your food processor. Process mixture until smooth, about 2 minutes.

Skim off the solid coconut cream portion from the top of each can of coconut milk and add it to the mixture. (Do not add liquid from the can, use only the solid coconut cream). Process until combined and smooth.

Take bottom layer out of the freezer and pour filling over prepared base.

Cover and place in the refrigerator to set overnight. If you are short on time, you can freeze for 2-3 hours, but overnight is best.

Once frozen, cut into 16 squares and serve. Cover and refrigerate leftovers. Photo shows a coconut garnish.

PEANUT BUTTER BLONDIES

MAKES
16 BLONDIES

PREHEAT
350°F

PREP TIME
15 MINUTES

COOK TIME
20-25 MINUTES

¾ cup peanut butter

1 small banana

¼ cup applesauce

14 medjool dates, pitted

¼ cup non-dairy milk of choice

2 teaspoons vanilla bean powder

1 teaspoon baking powder

1 teaspoon baking soda

2 cups oat flour

Preheat oven to 350 degrees F.

In a food processor, combine all ingredients except oat flour. Once thoroughly processed, scoop out of food processor with a large spoon and pour into a large bowl.

Mix in flour using a large mixing spoon. If need be, complete mixing with your hands. Dough will be a bit sticky, but you should have a nice dough once the flour is completely combined with the food processor ingredients.

Flatten dough in an 8x8 inch parchment-lined baking pan so that it is nice and even on top.

Bake for 20-25 minutes or until a fork or toothpick comes out clean. Remove from oven and let cool.

Once cooled, remove the blondies from pan and gently place on a large cutting board. Cut into 16 squares to serve.

OATMEAL BUTTERSCOTCH BLONDIES

MAKES
16 BLONDIES

PREHEAT
375°F

PREP TIME
15 MINUTES

COOK TIME
35 MINUTES

---

2 flaxseed "eggs"
(2 tablespoons ground
flaxseeds + ½ cup water)

3 teaspoons baking powder

¾ cup almond milk

2 tablespoons almond butter

¾ cup peanut butter

1½ tablespoon maca powder

3 very ripe medium-sized
bananas

15 medjool dates, pitted

1 tablespoon vanilla bean
powder

¾ cup almond flour

1½ tablespoon butterscotch
extract

2 cups rolled or old-fashioned
oats

1½ cups whole-wheat flour
or oat flour for gluten-free
version

Preheat oven to 375 degrees F.

Mix ground flaxseeds with ½ cup water in a small bowl or cup. Stir and let sit for a minute. In a food processor, add every ingredient (including flax "eggs") except for whole-wheat flour and oats and process until thoroughly combined.

Pour the processed mixture into a large bowl and add the whole-wheat flour and oats. Stir until the flour and oats have been thoroughly incorporated into the batter.

Pour the batter into a 9-inch parchment-lined baking pan and spread the top evenly with a large spoon. Sprinkle desired toppings on top.

Bake for 35 minutes or until blondies looks golden and center is cooked. Total baking time varies, so check every 5 minutes after 35 minutes.

CHOCOLATE SWEET POTATO SQUARES

MAKES
15 SQUARES

PREHEAT
350°F

PREP TIME*
15 MINUTES

COOK TIME
30 MINUTES

For the chocolate bottom layer

¾ cup vegan dark chocolate chips, melted

1 ½ cups oat flour

16 medjool dates, pitted

¾ cup cocoa powder

1 cup black beans (cooked, canned or boxed)

3 tablespoons cashew butter

½ cup almond flour

For the top sweet potato layer

4 medium-sized sweet potatoes (about 1 ½ cups), baked and peeled**

⅓ cup shredded coconut

8 medjool dates, pitted

1 teaspoon cinnamon

½ teaspoon nutmeg

Optional toppings

raspberries
shredded coconut

**To bake sweet potato, wrap in foil, and bake at 400°F for 45 minutes, until the sweet potato is tender enough to poke with a fork

Preheat oven to 350 degrees F.

To prepare chocolate bottom layer, melt dark chocolate chips in the microwave for 30 seconds, stir, and then heat for another 30 seconds. Add the melted chips to a food processor along with all of the other chocolate layer ingredients except the almond flour.

Pour the mixture into a large mixing bowl and add the almond flour. Using a large mixing spoon, mix the almond flour with the chocolate mixture. You may have to add a few tablespoons of water to moisten the mixture. Use your hands to mix in the almond flour well.

Form mixture into a dough ball and with your hands, flatten it out evenly on a parchment-lined 8x8 inch baking pan. The parchment paper will help you lift the squares out of the pan when they are finished baking. Place the chocolate bottom layer in the fridge for 10 minutes while you prepare the sweet potato layer.

Place the peeled and baked sweet potato into cleaned food processor along with the remaining sweet potato top layer ingredients and combine until thoroughly mixed. This should take a few minutes, pausing to scrape the sides with a spoon, until completely combined.

Take the chocolate bottom layer pan out of the fridge and pour the sweet potato layer on top. Spread it out evenly. Bake in the oven for 30 minutes and let it cool on cooling rack. Then place in the freezer for 20-30 minutes before slicing so that the squares can get firm, which makes slicing neater.

Decorate with fresh raspberries, shredded coconut or any other toppings you would like.

*Assumes sweet potatoes have already been baked.

RASPBERRY CHOCOLATE FROZEN BARS

MAKES
20 BARS

METHOD
FREEZE

PREP TIME
30 MINUTES

COOK TIME
NONE

For the chocolate pecan base

1 ½ cup raw pecan flour

1 cup almond flour

2 ½ teaspoons vanilla bean powder

10 medjool dates, pitted

1 ¼ cup cocoa powder

For the raspberry cashew cream filling

½ cup raw fresh cauliflower florets

⅓ cup cacao butter, melted

1 ½ teaspoon ground vanilla bean

1 ½ cup raw cashews, soaked overnight (or 1 cup raw, unsalted cashew butter)

10 medjool dates, pitted

2 cups fresh or defrosted frozen raspberries, preferably organic

2 Pitaya Plus dragon fruit smoothie packs for color* (optional)

For the chocolate top

¾ cup cocoa powder

1 cup peanut butter

2 very ripe medium-sized bananas

1 tablespoon ground vanilla bean

To prepare the chocolate pecan base, place pecan flour, almond flour, vanilla bean powder and pitted dates in a food processor and process thoroughly. Add the cocoa powder and process until completely combined. The result will be slightly crumbly. Press together with your hands and flatten it out in a layer on a tin-foil lined 8x8 inch baking pan. Place this layer in the refrigerator while you prepare the raspberry middle layer.

To prepare the raspberry cashew cream filling, place raw, fresh cauliflower florets in cleaned food processor and process until fine pieces form. Melt the cacao butter by placing it in a cup or small bowl and heating in the microwave for 45 seconds. Add the melted cacao butter to the food processor along with ground vanilla, cashews (or cashew butter), pitted dates and raspberries. Add pitaya packs (defrosted) if using. Process for a minute or so until all ingredients form a smooth and creamy mixture.

Take the chocolate pecan base out of the refrigerator and pour this raspberry mixture on top. Use a spoon to smooth the top of the raspberry layer. Place the pan back in the refrigerator while you prepare the final top layer.

To prepare the chocolate peanut butter top, clean your food processor and add all the remaining ingredients to it. You may need to stop and scrape down the sides before turning the food processor on again. The mixture will be somewhat thick. This is desirable.

Take the base out of the refrigerator and pour this final layer on top, smoothing and flattening with your hands. Freeze for at least one hour before decorating and cutting into slices. Store frozen and thaw just before serving. Top with strawberries, raspberries, or blueberries and/or chopped nut of your choice, if desired.

> *Pitaya is a synonym for dragon fruit and Pitaya Plus is the name of a company that makes organic frozen dragon fruit smoothie packs. You can find Pitaya Plus smoothie packs online and in many grocery and health food stores.

FUDGY AVO BARS

MAKES
15 BARS

METHOD
FREEZE

PREP TIME
18 MINUTES

COOK TIME
NONE

For the flaxseed date bottom

10 medjool dates, pitted

1 large, ripe banana

¼ cup ground flaxseeds

¼ cup raw almond butter

6 dried apricots, soaked with ¼ cup non-dairy milk of choice in advance

1 teaspoon vanilla bean powder

½ cup oat flour

For the avocado chocolate cream

10 medjool dates, pitted

½ large, ripe avocado

1½ teaspoon vanilla bean powder

½ cup black beans

¼ cup your favorite non-dairy milk

½ cup cocoa powder

Begin this recipe by soaking the apricots with non-dairy milk for at least 2-3 hours.

Add the dates to the food processor along with the banana, ground flaxseeds, almond butter, soaked apricot with soaking liquid and ground vanilla. Process until thoroughly mixed. Then add the oat flour and process until a smooth mixture forms.

Pour the mixture into a 8x8 inch baking pan. Smooth out the top and place this layer in the freezer so it can firm up. While the bottom layer is firming up, prepare the fudgy chocolate layer by blending all the other ingredients in this layer except for the cocoa powder. Process for a minute or so until all ingredients are well mixed. Then add the cocoa powder and process until the mixture is smooth and chocolaty.

Take the pan out of the freezer and pour the chocolaty layer on top, spreading it out evenly. Smooth the top and place it back in the freezer for at least 4 hours. Let it sit out of the freezer for about 15 minutes before cutting into squares or slices. Decorate the tops with coconut shreds and/or fresh or frozen fruit if you wish.

RASPBERRY CHOCOLATE BARS

MAKES
16 BARS

METHOD
FREEZE

PREP TIME
NIGHT BEFORE &
20 MINUTES

COOK TIME
NONE

For the walnut-date crust

10 medjool dates, pitted

¾ cup raw walnuts

1 cup rolled or old-fashioned oats

½ cup almond flour

1 large, ripe banana

¼ cup non-dairy milk of choice

1 teaspoon cinnamon

1¼ teaspoons vanilla bean powder

For the cashew cream filling

2 cans full-fat coconut milk,
refrigerated overnight, then
liquid removed*

1 cup raw cashew butter
(or 1¾ cup cashews, soaked in
water overnight)

10 medjool dates, pitted

juice of one lemon

1 tablespoon lemon zest

2 teaspoons vanilla bean powder

For the raspberry swirl

2 cups raspberries

*After refrigeration overnight, the
cream will have separated from
the liquid. Drain the liquid and set
aside, you will use only the cream
for this recipe.

Night before: refrigerate coconut milk

In a food processor or high-powered blender, process the dates and walnuts together first. Then add the rest of the crust ingredients and process until a nice dough is formed. The dough will be firm, but a bit sticky which is what you want. Press the dough together with your hands and mold it into an 8x8 inch baking pan until it spreads across the entire bottom of the pan. Flatten it out evenly and place it in the freezer while you prepare the filling.

To prepare cashew cream filling, skim off the solid "cream" portion in each can of coconut milk. Place the coconut cream, cashew butter, dates, lemon, zest and vanilla in a food processor and process until completely smooth. (If you are using soaked cashews, process them first before adding the other ingredients) If needed, add a few tablespoons of the liquid portion of the coconut milk to assist in processing. Once completely processed and a smooth cream forms (it will be liquidy and this is okay), take the bottom layer out of the freezer and pour this mixture on top.

To prepare the raspberry swirl topping, place the raspberries in the cleaned food processor and blend well. Spoon the raspberry topping mixture onto the top of the other two layers. Using a sharp knife, begin to make swirls or "figure eights" into the cashew cream layer to achieve that swirly look.

Place the pan into the freezer to firm up for at least 3 hours before removing from pan, slicing into 15 bars and serving.

The crust is easy to prepare and contains just seven ingredients, but what makes these special is the cashew cream filling and raspberry swirl. If you are feeling artsy, you can get decorative with the raspberry swirl topping.

BREAKFAST SUPERFOOD KALE BARS

MAKES
12 BARS

PREHEAT
250°F

PREP TIME
30 MINUTES

COOK TIME
40-45 MINUTES

1 cup chopped kale (packed into the cup), tough stems and center ribs removed

12 medjool dates, pitted

1 cup peanut butter (or nut butter of choice)

1 teaspoon vanilla bean powder

2 tablespoons ground flaxseeds

1½ cup rolled or old-fashioned oats

3 tablespoons chia seeds

3 tablespoons sunflower seeds

3 tablespoons shredded coconut

⅓ cup dried cherries, organic raisins, goji berries or other dried fruit

½ cup fresh or thawed frozen corn

1 cup non-dairy milk of choice

Preheat oven to 250 degrees F.

Line an 8×8 inch baking pan with parchment paper. Mix medjool dates, peanut butter, vanilla bean powder, ground flaxseeds, corn and milk in a food processor or blender.

In a large bowl, combine the oats, seeds, shredded coconut, goji berries (or other dried fruit); mix thoroughly. Add peanut butter/date/corn mixture to the bowl and stir until well coated. Add in chopped kale and chocolate chips (if desired) and mix evenly into the mixture.

Transfer the mixture and press it firmly into the prepared pan spreading it evenly. Bake for 40-45 minutes. Let cool for at least 20 minutes. Cut and serve.

Each time you take a bite of one of these delicious bars, remember that every ingredient prevents disease in its own unique way.

These bars store wonderfully in the freezer, just heat for a minute in the microwave to defrost, or store in the fridge. I prefer to eat these bars heated, but room temperature is great too.

MATCHA MARATHON SQUARES

MAKES
16 BARS

PREHEAT
350°F

PREP TIME
25 MINUTES

COOK TIME
25 MINUTES

½ cup white rice, cooked

¼ cup raw cashew butter

¼ cup hemp seeds

14 large medjool dates, pitted

1 teaspoon vanilla bean powder

1 medium-sized, ripe banana

3 tablespoons matcha powder

2 tablespoons maca powder

1 cup oat flour

½ cup 85% dark chocolate chips or organic raisins (optional)

Preheat oven to 350 degrees F.

Prepare the white rice according to its package directions. Let the white rice cool in a mixing bowl.

Add cooled rice to a food processor along with the cashew butter - room temperature cashew butter works best – hemp seeds, pitted medjool dates, and vanilla bean powder. Process well, until all ingredients form a smooth mixture.

Then add the banana, matcha powder, maca powder and oat flour and process those in until a smooth, even mixture forms. It will be slightly thick. This is desirable. Pour the mixture into a mixing bowl and mix in dark chocolate chips or raisins, if desired.

Flatten out mixture in a parchment-lined 8x8 inch square baking pan as you would brownies and place the pan in the oven. Bake for 25 minutes. Allow them to cool for at least 15 minutes before slicing into bars.

I don't use white rice often, but for these bars it was the perfect choice because when running long distances or for a marathon or triathlon, food that sustains energy while not containing too much fiber is essential. This is the only recipe in the book I purposely did not prioritize high-fiber ingredients. No runner wants stomach problems in the middle of a race. Hence, below you will find the perfect combination of ingredients to keep any runner satiated yet comfortable.

Breads

CHAPTER 3

"People tend to be generous when sharing their nonsense, fear, and ignorance.
And while they seem quite eager to feed you their negativity, please remember
that sometimes the diet we need to be on is a spiritual and emotional one.
Be cautious with what you feed your mind and soul. Fuel yourself with positivity
and let that fuel propel you into positive action."
– Steve Maraboli

The turbulent turns and the tides that twist them.
You may think not of some things you now possess.
Be it a lover, abundant food, or a friend with an
ebullient mood.

Some of these things may last,
but some of them may come to pass.

All of the joys brought to you,
may not forever ensue.

But some of them will, until your last day.
It is being wise about what you let stay.

CHOCOLATE PEANUT BUTTER BREAD

MAKES
12 SLICES

PREHEAT
350°F

PREP TIME
15 MINUTES

COOK TIME
35 MINUTES

2 flax "eggs"
(2 tablespoons ground flaxseeds + ½ cup of your favorite non-dairy milk)

18 medjool dates, pitted

3 medium-sized, ripe bananas

¾ cup cocoa powder

1 tablespoon ground vanilla bean powder

⅓ cup peanut butter

2 teaspoons baking powder

1 teaspoon cinnamon

½ teaspoon nutmeg

½ cup almond flour

1½ cup oat flour

Optional toppings

melted dark chocolate

fresh or frozen cherries or strawberries

pumpkin seeds or favorite nuts, seeds

shredded coconut

Preheat oven to 350 degrees F.

In a cup or small bowl, mix ground flaxseeds with non-dairy milk to form two flax "eggs." Stir and let sit for a minute.

Add dates, bananas, cocoa powder, vanilla, peanut butter and baking powder. Process for a minute or so until a smooth, creamy mixture forms.

Add the cinnamon, nutmeg, almond flour, oat flour and mix. Pour the dough into a parchment-lined bread pan, add any of your favorite toppings on top.

Bake for 35 minutes or until you can poke the top with a fork and the fork comes out clean.

RASPBERRY VANILLA BREAD

MAKES
12 SLICES

PREHEAT
350°F

PREP TIME
15 MINUTES

COOK TIME
1 HOUR

Wet ingredients

2 flax "eggs"
(2 tablespoons ground
flaxseeds + ½ cup
non-dairy milk)

3 ripe bananas, peeled

1 cup canned white beans

12 medjool dates, pitted

1 tablespoon vanilla extract

1 teaspoon vanilla bean powder

Dry ingredients

2 cups whole-wheat flour

½ cup almond flour

1 teaspoon baking powder

1 teaspoon baking soda

1 teaspoon cinnamon

1 teaspoon nutmeg

1 cup fresh or frozen raspberries

½ cup organic raisins

Preheat oven to 350 degrees F.

Add all wet ingredients to a food processor and blend until smooth and creamy. Put aside.

In a large mixing bowl, sift together flours, baking powder, baking soda, cinnamon and nutmeg. Stir in wet ingredients and mix and knead with hands until a nice dough is formed.

Add a few tablespoons more non-dairy milk, if necessary. Knead in raisins.

Separate the dough into two equal parts. Place each part into two parchment-lined loaf pans, flattening out the tops.

Poke in raspberries with the handle of a wooden spoon.

Bake for one hour or until an inserted toothpick comes out clean.

PUMPKIN DOUGH BREAD

MAKES
12 SLICES

PREHEAT
350°F

PREP TIME
15 MINUTES

COOK TIME
40-45 MINUTES

2 flax "eggs"
  (2 tablespoons ground
  flaxseeds + ½ cup non-dairy
  milk or water)

15 medjool dates, pitted

1 (15 oz.) can white beans or
  garbanzo beans

1 cup mashed pumpkin or sweet
  potato (baked or from a can)

1 ripe large banana

2 teaspoons baking powder

1 ½ teaspoon vanilla bean
  powder

1 teaspoon cinnamon

½ teaspoon nutmeg

1 teaspoon pumpkin pie spice

½ cup almond flour

1 ½ cup oat or spelt flour

1 cup rolled or old-fashioned
  oats

½ cup dark chocolate chips
  or organic raisins

Preheat oven to 350 degrees F.

Line a 9x5 loaf pan with tin foil or parchment paper. In a cup or small bowl, mix ground flaxseeds with water to create flax "eggs." Let sit for a minute.

Add the flax "eggs" to a food processor along with all other ingredients except for the oat flour (or spelt), oats and raisins.

Process for a few minutes until a smooth mixture is formed. The mixture should have a pudding-like consistency and be somewhat thick.

Pour this mixture into a large bowl and mix in the oat flour (or spelt), whole oats, and dark chocolate chips or raisins, mixing all ingredients in evenly.

Separate the dough into two equal parts and scoop each one into a parchment-lined loaf pan and top with additional dark chocolate chips or raisins, if desired.

Bake for 40-45 minutes or until you can stick a fork or toothpick in the center and it comes out clean.

Remove the pan from the oven and let the bread set for at least 20 minutes before transferring to a plate to cool. Let cool completely before slicing, preferably for several hours, otherwise it will be sticky/crumbly when slicing.

COCONUT BANANA BREAD

MAKES
12 SERVINGS

PREHEAT
350°F

PREP TIME
10 MINUTES

COOK TIME
55 MINUTES

- 3 very ripe bananas + 1 for decorative topping
- 3 flax "eggs" (3 tablespoons ground flaxseeds + ½ cup nondairy milk of choice)
- 10 medjool dates, pitted
- 2 heaping tablespoons coconut butter (can substitute cashew butter)
- 1½ teaspoon ground vanilla bean
- 2 teaspoons cinnamon
- 1 teaspoon nutmeg
- 3 teaspoons baking powder
- 1 cup almond flour
- 2 cups oat flour
- coconut flakes for topping (optional)
- unsweetened baking dark chocolate for topping (optional)

Preheat oven to 350 degrees F.

Mix the ground flaxseeds with the nondairy milk. Set aside for a minute or so to form flax "eggs."

Add the three bananas to the food processor and process with all ingredients except almond and oat flour. Process until completely combined.

Add almond flour and process that in thoroughly. Lastly, add oat flour and process until a nice, evenly mixed batter is formed.

Pour the batter into a parchment paper lined loaf pan. If using toppings, add those. To use the dark chocolate topping, heat hardened chocolate in the microwave for a minute, stir and then using a spoon, pour melted chocolate on top.

Bake for 55 minutes or until the loaf is golden brown on top. Let cool.

Even with a mediocre diet, flaxseeds provide powerful protection against breast cancer. Another interesting study on flax followed women for up to 10 years and found a 51% reduced risk of all-cause mortality, and a 71% reduced risk of breast cancer mortality.[1]

Zucchini (Cucurbita pepo) is a popular variety of summer squash that can be consumed raw or cooked. The flower of the zucchini plant is edible. Fried squash blossoms are considered a delicacy.

Nutrients and vitamins found in zucchini can help prevent cancer and heart disease. Zucchinis, especially golden skin varieties, are rich in flavonoid polyphenolic antioxidants such as carotenes, lutein, and zeaxanthin. These compounds help scavenge harmful oxygen-derived free radicals and reactive oxygen species (ROS) from the body that play a role in aging and various disease processes. Surprisingly, a zucchini has more potassium than a banana.[2,3]

ZUCCHINI BREAD

MAKES
12 SLICES

PREHEAT
350ºF

PREP TIME
30 MINUTES

COOK TIME
2 HOURS

---

2 flax "eggs"
(2 heaping tablespoons
ground flaxseeds + ½ cup
non-diary milk)

2 medium zucchinis

3 tablespoons frozen corn

14 medjool dates, pitted

2 teaspoons baking powder

1 teaspoon baking soda

1 ½ teaspoon vanilla bean
powder

1 ½ teaspoon ground cinnamon

1 teaspoon ground nutmeg

1 teaspoon ground ginger

½ cup raw pecans or walnuts

3 cups oat flour

Preheat oven to 350 degrees F.

Take the corn kernels out of the freezer and let thaw. Line a 9x5 inch loaf pan with parchment paper. While the oven is being preheated, in a cup or small bowl, mix the ground flaxseeds with non-dairy milk to prepare the flax "eggs." Stir and let sit for a minute or so.

Add the zucchini to a food processor and process until a paste forms. Add the corn to the food processor along with the flax "eggs."

Pit medjool dates and soften them by soaking in water and heating them in the microwave for 30 seconds. Completely drain-off water and add to the food processor along with baking powder, baking soda, vanilla, cinnamon, nutmeg and ginger. Process for a minute or so until all ingredients have been thoroughly mixed and the result is smooth and creamy. Add raw pecans or walnuts and 1½ cup of the oat flour to the food processor and process for a few more minutes until both have been completely incorporated into the batter. Then add the last 1½ cup oat flour to the food processor and process that in as well. It is best to add the oat flour in gradually for easier processing.

Pour the bread batter into a parchment-lined loaf pan. Bake for 2 hours or until a toothpick inserted into the center comes out clean. Allow the bread to cool in the loaf pan for 15 minutes before transferring it to a wire rack to cool for 20 minutes before slicing with a sharp, serrated knife.

The bread will last for 5-7 days if stored in the refrigerator and as long as 2-3 months if stored in the freezer. I love slicing the bread before freezing it and then defrost individual slices, either by lightly toasting them or defrosting in the microwave.

CHAI SPICE CORNBREAD

MAKES
11 MUFFINS

PREHEAT
350°F

PREP TIME*
15 MINUTES

COOK TIME
30 MINUTES

2 flax "eggs"
(2 tablespoons ground flaxseeds + ½ cup non-dairy milk)

1 cup cornmeal

½ cup oat flour

½ cup almond flour

2 teaspoons baking powder

1 teaspoon baking soda

18 medjool dates, pitted

1 cup baked and peeled sweet potato*

1 cup frozen corn kernels

½ cup raw cashew butter

1 teaspoon cinnamon

½ teaspoon nutmeg

¼ teaspoon cloves

*To bake sweet potato, heat oven to 400 degrees F. Wrap each sweet potato in foil, place on a baking tray, and bake for one hour. You should be able to easily poke a fork into the sweet potato.

Preheat oven to 350 degrees F.

To prepare the flax "eggs" mix the ground flaxseeds with non-dairy milk in a cup or small bowl. Stir and let sit for a minute or so.

Combine cornmeal, oat flour, baking soda and baking powder in a large bowl. Stir well and set the bowl aside.

In a high-powered blender, combine cashew butter, medjool dates, flax "eggs" with their liquid, sweet potato and all spices. Then combine and mix with the dry ingredient in the large bowl. Add in the frozen corn kernels. You don't have to defrost the corn kernels before adding them.

Pour the batter into a paper-lined muffin pan. Bake for 30 minutes or until the top has a golden tinge. Allow to cool 10-15 minutes before serving.

*Assumes sweet potato is already baked.

APPLE PIE MUFFINS

MAKES
10 MUFFINS

PREHEAT
350°F

PREP TIME
12 MINUTES

COOK TIME
18 MINUTES

2 flax "eggs"
(2 tablespoons ground
flaxseeds + ½ cup
non-dairy milk)

15 medjool dates, pitted

2 medium-sized, very ripe
(speckled) bananas

2 organic apples or pears,
diced into small pieces

½ cup applesauce, no sugar
added

2 tablespoons raw cashew butter

1 ¼ cup almond flour

1 cup whole-wheat flour
or oat flour

1 tablespoon cinnamon

1 teaspoon nutmeg

2 teaspoons baking powder

1 tablespoon arrowroot powder

Preheat oven to 350 degrees F.

In a cup or small bowl, mix ground flaxseeds with non-dairy milk to create flax "eggs." Let this mixture sit for a couple of minutes. Set aside.

Soften dates by soaking them in water and heating in a microwave for 30 seconds. Drain the water and add the dates to food processor with the flax "eggs," bananas, applesauce, raw cashew butter, spices, baking powder and arrowroot. Process until smooth and creamy.

Add almond flour and process until smooth. Then add whole-wheat flour (or oat flour) and again, process until smooth. Pour the dough into a large mixing bowl. Add in desired amount of diced apple (or pear) and stir into the batter evenly.

Place baking cups in a muffin tin and spoon in muffin batter. You can make medium-sized muffins by filling the cups three quarters of the way or make larger muffins by filling cups all the way up.

Bake for 18 minutes or until you can place a fork or toothpick on top and it comes out clean. Let cool for at least 10 minutes.

"Clarity about what matters provides clarity about what does not."

~Cal Newport, Deep Work: Rules for Focused Success in a Distracted World

Successful people most often work hard. They typically work very, very hard. This almost always equates to years and years of hard work and diligent practice. My views about passion and success changed after reading, So Good They Can't Ignore You: Why Skills Trump Passion In the Quest for Work You Love by Cal Newport. I wish the hustle was as easy as the dream, but as I type this, I realize that all of the hard work that goes into anything special is actually part of the dream itself. If you love something enough, you will be willing to put in the hard work it takes to make your dream a reality.

TROPICAL CARROT CAKE MUFFINS

MAKES
12 MUFFINS

PREHEAT
350°F

PREP TIME
NIGHT BEFORE &
25 MINUTES

COOK TIME
30 MINUTES

For the muffins

1 cup whole-wheat flour
or oat flour

½ cup oat flour

2 teaspoons baking powder

1 cup medjool dates, pitted and
softened

1 cup dried pineapple, softened
in advance with a small
amount of water

1 ½ cups grated carrots

½ cup unsweetened dried
coconut

1 teaspoon ground cinnamon

1 teaspoon ground nutmeg

3 tablespoons ground flaxseeds

½ cup organic raisins

For optional whipped cream icing

1 (15 oz.) can full-fat coconut
milk, refrigerated overnight,
then liquid removed*

4 medjool dates, pitted

1 teaspoon vanilla bean powder

*After refrigeration overnight, the
cream will have separated from
the liquid. Drain the liquid and
set aside, you will use only the
cream for this recipe.

Night before: refrigerate coconut milk, soak pineapple

Preheat oven to 350 degrees F.

To make the muffins, soak pineapple in water for at least a few hours, but ideally overnight. Then drain pineapple of water. Combine all the ingredients (except the grated carrots and optional raisins) in a food processor and pulse until it's all in small pieces and sticks together. Pour the batter into a large bowl and evenly mix in the grated carrots and optional raisins.

Use baking cups in the muffin tin and roll dough into 2-inch circles. Place each one in a muffin tin and flatten the tops. Bake for 30 minutes or until an inserted toothpick comes out clean.

To make the whipped cream icing, soften medjool dates by soaking them in water in a small bowl. Heat them in the microwave for 30 seconds. Remove them from the water and add them to a large mixing bowl along with the ground vanilla.

Remove the can of coconut milk from the refrigerator and skim off the solid 'cream' portion at the top. Place the cream portion into a medium mixing bowl.

Use an electric hand mixer or a stand mixer (fitted with the whisk attachment) to beat the coconut cream with the softened dates and vanilla on medium until light, fluffy and soft peaks form or do this in a food processor.

The icing will be thin now, but firms up a bit upon chilling. Chill for about 4 hours. The icing will still be creamy, soft and smooth. Add to the top of the muffins.

Each time I prepare these tropical treats filled with carrot cake delight, memories of enjoyed times past arrive with abundant might. I love when classic foods can remind us of times once treasured, recollections of those moments gastronomically pleasured.

There once was a child who loved her peanut butter and jelly bliss,
after school she ate them upon giving her mother a welcoming kiss.
She swung on swings and relished the rain,
with bruises from playing rough her only pain.

Sometimes it feels like just yesterday,
that she was that child, just a kid at play.
Time can travel fast her adult self thought,
now a woman with experience only time has taught.

Regardless of age, be it in forties, eighties and above,
Antioxidants for the heart will be optimism, joy and love,
A thought to remember, a treasure often the solution,
is our inner child is always inside waiting for a reunion.

PEANUT BUTTER AND JELLY MUFFINS

MAKES
16 MUFFINS

PREHEAT
350°F

PREP TIME
25 MINUTES

COOK TIME
20 MINUTES

2 flax "eggs"
(2 tablespoons flaxseeds +
½ cup non-dairy milk)

12 medjool dates, pitted

2 ripe bananas

½ cup unsweetened applesauce

½ cup peanut butter

1 ½ teaspoon vanilla bean
powder

1 cup walnut flour
(ground up raw walnuts)

2 cups spelt flour
(or whole-wheat flour or
oat flour or a combination
of these)

1 teaspoon baking powder

About ½ cup of your favorite jam
(I used unsweetened organic
strawberry)

Preheat oven to 350 degrees F.

Line two muffin pans with muffin cups. You will likely need 16 cups. In a small bowl or cup, stir ground flaxseeds in non-dairy milk to form flax "eggs." Set aside.

In a food processor or high-powered blender, combine the first six ingredients, including the flax "eggs," and blend until all ingredients are completely mixed and a smooth peanut butter cream is formed. Set aside. In a large mixing bowl, combine walnut flour, spelt flour and baking powder.

Add the blended ingredients to the dry ingredients and stir well until all of the flour is thoroughly incorporated into the mixture. Fill each muffin cup half full with peanut butter batter (about 2 tablespoons). Then spoon about one tablespoon of jelly on top of each filled cup.

Spoon the leftover batter over jelly, making sure to cover each muffin completely to prevent the jelly from bubbling out of the muffins. However, do not panic if muffins are not completely covered because bubbling out will simply result in slightly messy, yet delicious muffins.

Bake for 20 minutes or until the muffins spring back when touched lightly in the center. Remove from the oven and let them cool for a least five minutes.

CARAMEL CHOCOLATE CHIP MUFFINS

MAKES
12 MUFFINS

PREHEAT
350°F

PREP TIME
15 MINUTES

COOK TIME
45 MINUTES

3 flax "eggs"
(3 tablespoons ground
flaxseeds + ¾ cup
almond milk)

3 tablespoons raw cashew butter

2 ripe bananas

15 medjool dates, pitted

1 tablespoon maca powder

½ cup canned white beans,
liquid removed

1 teaspoon vanilla bean powder

1 teaspoon baking powder

1 teaspoon baking soda

2 cups oat flour

1 cup vegan 85% dark
chocolate chips

Preheat oven to 350 degrees F.

Line a muffin tray with baking cups. Add all ingredients except for oat flour and chocolate chips into a food processor and process until thoroughly combined.

Gradually add oat flour one cup at a time, processing to incorporate into the mix before adding more of the flour mixture.

Add the other cup of oat flour until all the ingredients are mixed well and the batter is smooth.

Once the oat flour has been incorporated, pour the dough into a large mixing bowl. Stir in the dark chocolate chips. Divide batter evenly between muffin cups for a total of 12 muffins. Bake approximately 45 minutes depending on oven heat.

The muffins will be ready when the tops spring back after being touched. Allow them to cool for at least 15 minutes before removing from the muffin tin.

LEMON POPPY SEED MUFFINS

MAKES
12 MUFFINS

PREHEAT
350ºF

PREP TIME
15 MINUTES

COOK TIME
20-25 MINUTES

2 flax "eggs"
(2 heaping tablespoons
ground flaxseeds + ½ cup
non-dairy milk)

2 teaspoons baking powder

½ cup almond flour

1 cup oat flour

1 cup whole-wheat flour
(or more oat flour)

3 tablespoons poppy seeds

2 tablespoons lemon juice

1 teaspoon lemon extract
(optional)

2 tablespoons almond butter

12 medjool dates, pitted

Preheat oven to 350 degrees F.

Line a standard muffin tin with paper liners. In a large mixing bowl, use a large spoon or spatula and combine dry ingredients: baking powder, oat, almond and whole-wheat flours and poppy seeds. Set aside.

Mix ground flaxseeds with non-dairy milk and let sit for a minute. In a food processor, process flax "eggs," medjool dates, lemon juice, lemon extract (optional) and almond butter until thoroughly combined. Then, mix thoroughly with the dry ingredients.

Bake for 20-25 minutes or until a toothpick inserted in the center comes out clean.

SUPERFOOD CHOCOLATE MUFFINS

MAKES
16 MUFFINS

PREHEAT
350°F

PREP TIME
15 MINUTES

COOK TIME
25 MINUTES

For the very vanilla batter

1 (15 oz.) can white beans

2 cups rolled or old-fashioned oats

½ cup applesauce or one ripe banana

3 tablespoons coconut butter

½ cup coconut flour or almond flour

12 medjool dates, pitted

1 teaspoon vanilla bean powder

1 ½ teaspoon baking powder

For the creamy dark chocolate batter

1 (15 oz.) can black beans

1 cup cocoa powder

10 medjool dates, pitted

½ cup water

Preheat oven to 350 degrees F.

Line two muffin tins with paper muffin/cupcake cups.

Prepare the very vanilla batter first. Place all beans and 1 cup of the oats (not all of the oats) in a food processor and process well. Make sure to drain the beans and not add any liquid from the can.

Next add applesauce (or banana) and coconut butter and process until combined. Add the rest of the ingredients, including the last cup of oats and process until a nice batter forms.

To prepare the dark chocolate batter, place all ingredients in your cleaned food processor and process. Again, make sure to drain the beans from the can before you add them to the food processor.

The chocolaty result will be smooth and somewhat thin. It will be thinner than the vanilla batter. Pour the chocolate batter into a bowl and then you will be ready to mold the batter into muffins.

With your hands, mold the vanilla dough into balls about one-inch diameter. Keep some extra dough for creating a nice vanilla swirl or your own pattern on top.

Place the vanilla dough balls into the muffin tin and flatten. Top with some of the chocolate batter. Make sure that the dough fills the muffin tin only half way. Create vanilla swirls on top (see photo) by rolling some of the vanilla dough into strips and placing on top of the chocolate in a swirl shape.

Bake for 25 minutes and let cool for at least 15 minutes once you take them out of the oven.

Beans are the ideal substitution for oil in many muffin, bread, cookie and cake recipes. And look at all of the additional healthy, delectable ingredients in this recipe.

If using quinoa, let me tell you a little about it. Each grain of quinoa (unless pre-washed) is covered in a soapy substance called saponin. It tastes bitter and will affect the taste of your quinoa if you don't remove it.

To remove the saponin:
First measure the quinoa and put it into a large bowl. Fill it with clean water. Let it soak for a little while. Then, using a whisk, swish the quinoa around until you see a soapy residue come out of the quinoa. You might have to do this for a few minutes to get all the saponin off. Once the soapy residue is off, strain the quinoa. Now you have saponins-free wet quinoa.

SUNFLOWER COCONUT MUFFINS

MAKES
15 MUFFINS

PREHEAT
375°F

PREP TIME
15-20 MINUTES

COOK TIME
20 MINUTES

2 flax "eggs"
(2 tablespoons ground flaxseeds + ½ cup non-dairy milk)

2 teaspoons baking powder

1 cup toasted quinoa (optional)

⅓ cup raw sunflower seeds

⅓ cup unsweetened shredded coconut (or flakes)

2 ripe bananas

2 tablespoons coconut or cashew butter

⅓ cup canned white beans

12 medjool dates, pitted

½ cup almond flour

1 cup whole-wheat flour or oat flour

1 cup blueberries or strawberries finely sliced or freeze dried

Preheat oven to 375 degrees F.

Line a muffin tin with baking cups. Mix and stir ground flaxseeds and non-dairy milk to make flax "eggs." Add baking soda to the flax "eggs" and put the mixture into a medium-sized mixing bowl and let sit for a few minutes. Set aside.

Toast the wet quinoa by adding it into a large-enough pan and use a medium low heat. Use a whisk to move it around. Once you see that it is lightly dried out and just a little brown, it's done. This takes about 15 minutes. It will make slight popping sounds as it approaches being done. To best ascertain doneness, scoop out a teaspoon, cool it slightly, and taste it. It should have a slightly nutty flavor. Place the quinoa in a large bowl along with the sunflower seeds, berries and coconut flakes. Mix and set aside.

In a food processor, combine flax "eggs" mixture with bananas, white beans, dates, almond flour and whole-wheat flour. Process until a nice evenly mixed dough is formed. Pour into a large mixing bowl.

Add the toasted quinoa-sunflower seed and berries to the mixture in the large bowl containing the dough and mix well. Divide the batter evenly between muffin tins. Each cup in the tin should be about ¾ of the way full. Sprinkle the tops of each muffin with a bit more sunflower seeds and/or coconut flakes.

Bake for 20 minutes or until a toothpick inserted into the center comes out clean and the edges are golden brown. Let cool for at least 10 minutes in the pan, then gently remove and let muffins cool completely on a cooling rack. Don't try to remove the muffin paper before they are completely cooled because they will stick to the paper.

MACADAMIA GINGER PEAR MUFFINS

MAKES
10 MUFFINS

PREHEAT
350°F

PREP TIME
12 MINUTES

COOK TIME
18 MINUTES

3 flax "eggs"
(3 tablespoons flaxseeds +
¾ cup non-dairy milk)

14 medjool dates, pitted

¼ cup macadamia nut butter or
ground macadamia nuts

½ cup applesauce

1 teaspoon lemon juice

2 teaspoons baking powder

1 teaspoon ground ginger

½ teaspoon cinnamon

½ teaspoon nutmeg

½ cup almond flour

1 cup spelt flour

1 cup whole-wheat flour

3 ripe pears or apples, chopped

Preheat oven to 350 degrees F.

Mix ground flaxseeds in non-dairy milk, stir and let sit for a couple of minutes so it can form flax "eggs."

Add the flax "eggs" and pitted dates to a food processor along with all other ingredients except for the spelt and whole-wheat flour. Process for a minute or so until evenly mixed.

Pour mixture into a large bowl and stir in both remaining flours. Once a nice smooth batter forms, stir in chopped pear chunks and any other fruit (fresh or dried) you would like.

Pour the batter into lined muffin tins, filling batter just below the top of each tin. The muffins will rise while baking.

Bake them for 18 minutes or until you can stick a toothpick or fork in the top and it comes out clean.

Let them cool for at least 10 minutes before enjoying.

Almonds provide double-barrel protection against diabetes and cardiovascular disease. Almonds decrease post-meal rises in blood sugar. The high antioxidant content in nuts is another reason to explain results seen in the Iowa Women's Health Study in which risk of death from cardiovascular and coronary heart diseases showed strong and consistent reductions with increasing nut consumption. Total death rates decreased 11 percent and 19 percent for nut/peanut butter intake once per week and 1-4 times per week, respectively.

Even though a handful of nuts is about 180 calories, those who eat almonds habitually do not consume more calories or weigh more. In one study, all participants ate the same breakfast, then 0, 173 or 259 calories worth of almonds as a snack, then ate as much as they wanted for the rest of the day. Those who ate the nuts were so satisfied that they ate less for lunch and dinner, so that by the end of the day, there was no significant difference in total calorie intake between any of the three groups.[4-6]

Blueberries have been shown to improve memory and other measures of brain function in studies on both children and adults. They contain large amounts of anthocyanins and tannins, types of antioxidants linked to the reversal and prevention of age-related mental decline. Researchers have found that eating blueberries is a preventive measure for optimal cognitive functioning later in life.[7]

Flaxseeds strongly help prevent breast cancer and blueberries are brain food. To read more about the health benefits of flaxseeds and more interesting almond nutrition facts, head to the recipe on page 99 for Coconut Banana Bread.

BLUEBERRY BANANA MUFFINS

MAKES
12 MUFFINS

PREHEAT
350°F

PREP TIME
15 MINUTES

COOK TIME
35-40 MINUTES

3 flax "eggs"
(3 tablespoons ground
flaxseeds + ¾ cup
non-dairy milk)

2 teaspoons baking powder

½ cup toasted quinoa

⅓ cup raw sunflower seeds,
slightly chopped

⅓ cup unsweetened shredded
coconut

1 cup fresh or frozen blueberries,
defrosted; save ¼ for garnish

2 ripe bananas

2 tablespoons corn kernels

12 medjool dates, pitted

½ cup almond flour

1 cup whole-wheat flour
or oat flour

Preheat oven to 350 degrees F.

Line a muffin tin with baking cups. Mix the non-dairy milk and ground flaxseeds in a small mixing bowl or cup and let sit for a couple of minutes so it can form flax "eggs." Set aside.

To prepare toasted quinoa, add the quinoa and 2 tablespoons of water into a large nonstick skillet over medium-high heat, and stir the quinoa occasionally, until it is lightly dried out and toasted, about 15 minutes. Stir it enough so that it doesn't stick to the pan. It will make slight popping sounds as it approaches being done. Mix the quinoa in a large bowl with the sunflower seeds, and coconut flakes.

In a food processor, combine the flax "eggs," bananas, corn kernels, dates, baking powder, almond flour and whole-wheat flour (or oat flour). Process until a nice evenly mixed dough is formed.

Add the toasted quinoa-sunflower seed mixture to the large bowl containing the dough and mix in well. Add blueberries by folding them in.

Divide the batter evenly between muffin tins about ¾ of the way full. Sprinkle the tops of each muffin with the rest of the blueberries.

Bake for 35-40 minutes or until a toothpick inserted into the center comes out clean and the edges are golden brown. Don't try to remove the muffin cups before they are completely cooled because they will stick to the paper.

CHOCOLATE DREAM MUFFINS

MAKES
14 MUFFINS

PREHEAT
350°F

PREP TIME
12 MINUTES

COOK TIME
30 MINUTES

2 chia "eggs"
(2 tablespoons ground chia seeds + ½ cup non-dairy milk)

¼ cup Guinness (or rum)

12 medjool dates, pitted

2 ripe bananas

2 tablespoons apple cider vinegar and enough unsweetened soy milk to make ⅓ cup liquid

2 tablespoons raw cashew butter

1 teaspoon vanilla bean powder

½ cup cocoa powder

2½ cups rolled or old-fashioned oats

⅓ cup organic raisins

½ cup vegan 85% dark chocolate chips (optional)

Preheat oven to 350 degrees F.

Add baking cups to a muffin tin. Prepare chia "eggs" by mixing ground chia seeds in a small bowl or cup with non-dairy milk, stir and let sit for a minute to form a gel.

Add the Guinness (or rum) to the cup with the chia "eggs" and stir it in well. Pour the chia "eggs" mixture into a food processor along with all other ingredients except for the oats, raisins and optional chocolate chips. Process well.

Transfer the mixture into a large bowl. It will have a pudding-like consistency. Stir in rolled oats and chocolate chips and raisins evenly. Place into the fridge for at least one hour so it can get firm before pouring the batter into muffin tins. Top each unbaked muffin with dark chocolate chips, if desired.

Bake for 18 minutes, turn off the oven and allow the muffins to sit in the closed oven for another 12 or so minutes.

You can grind chia seeds in a high-powered blender or food processor. Ground chia seeds have a similar fine texture to ground flaxseeds.

CHOCOLATE BEET MUFFINS

MAKES
8 MUFFINS

PREHEAT
350°F

PREP TIME
12 MINUTES

COOK TIME
25 MINUTES

- 2 flax "eggs"
  (2 tablespoons ground
  flaxseeds + ½ cup
  non-dairy milk)
- 12 medjool dates, pitted
- 2 bananas
- 1 cup fresh or frozen strawberries
  or cherries (drain liquid if
  using frozen)
- ¾ cup beet puree
- 3 tablespoons coconut butter
- ½ cup unsweetened cocoa
  powder
- 1 tablespoon dark roast
  ground coffee)
- 2 teaspoons baking powder
- ½ cup almond flour
- ½ cup oat flour
- 1 cup whole-wheat flour
  (or more oat flour)
- ½ cup 85% dark chocolate chips
  (optional)

Preheat oven to 350 degrees F.

Line a muffin pan with baking cups. Stir ground flaxseeds with non-dairy milk and let sit for a couple of minutes so it can form flax "eggs."

Add flax "eggs," beet puree and coconut butter to a food processor and blend until smooth and creamy. Put aside.

In a large mixing bowl, sift together cocoa powder, coffee, baking powder, and flours. Stir in wet ingredients and mix thoroughly.

Place in the refrigerator for at least 30 minutes for dough to harden a bit.

Slice bananas and add to the batter. If using other fruit slices, add those too. Do not to add any extra liquid from the defrosted fruit, if using frozen.

Create muffin "dough balls" by rolling dough in your hands to form 2-inch dough balls. You should get between 7 to 9 dough balls to place in muffin tins.

Place in muffin pan and bake for 25 minutes or until a fork or toothpick inserted in the center comes out clean. Top with optional chocolate chips.

Curious about what beets taste like in muffins? Actually, you will not be able to taste them. The flavor of baked beets in muffins is so subtle that the sweet date, rich dark chocolate and fluffy floury goodness override any potential subtle flavors of those beets. The beets simply add more nutrition and their texture binds the muffins together much like the flax "eggs."

Pomegranate juice has been analyzed to have greater antioxidant capacity than red wine, grape juice, cranberry juice, green tea and acai juice.

Multiple studies have shown that pomegranate's potent antioxidant capacity may provide significant protection against heart disease, cancer and cognitive impairment.

Pomegranate has anti-angiogenic properties, meaning that they may help to prevent growing tumors from acquiring a blood supply, preventing those tumors from receiving the nutrients that would allow them to grow larger.

Pomegranate is also one of the few foods (mushrooms are another) that contain natural aromatase inhibitors. This means that they inhibit the production of estrogen, which can reduce breast cancer risk.[8,9]

SUPERFOOD BERRY MUFFINS

MAKES
8 MUFFINS

PREHEAT
350°F

PREP TIME
12 MINUTES

COOK TIME
18 MINUTES

2 flax "eggs"
(2 heaping tablespoons
ground flaxseeds + ½ cup
non-dairy milk)

2 teaspoons baking powder

½ cup canned white beans

1 very ripe, large banana

1 tablespoon coconut butter

12 medjool dates, pitted

1 teaspoon vanilla bean powder

1 teaspoon almond extract
(optional)

½ cup almond flour

½ cup oat flour

¾ cup whole-wheat flour

1 cup fresh or frozen
pomegranates or berries
(a mixture of both, if desired)

½ cup 85% dark chocolate chips
(optional)

¼ cup sunflower seeds (optional)

Preheat oven to 350 degrees F.

Line a muffin tin with baking cups. In a cup or small bowl, stir ground flaxseeds with non-dairy milk and let sit for a couple of minutes so it can form flax "eggs." Mix together flax "eggs" and baking powder. Stir and let sit for a minute.

Add all ingredients except for almond flour, oat flour, whole-wheat flour, pomegranates (or berries) and chocolate chips to a food processor (this includes the flax "eggs" mixture). Process until the mixture is completely blended and smooth.

Pour the batter into a large mixing bowl and stir in almond flour, oat flour and whole-wheat flour. Mix until flours are thoroughly combined with the blended mixture and a nice dough is formed.

Stir in pomegranates or if using, berries, sunflower seeds and/or dark chocolate chips and mix them evenly throughout the batter.

Using a medium- to small-sized spoon, pour the batter into the muffin tins until each tin is about ¾ full.

Bake for approximately 18 minutes or until the muffins have a slightly golden crust and are firm on the inside. Allow the muffins to cool for 10 minutes on a cooling rack before serving. Add optional chocolate chips to the top for garnish.

CHAPTER 4

"You can't go back and change the beginning,
but you can start where you are
and change the ending."
– C.S. Lewis

Only the present filled her mind.
A past of toil and struggle she deftly left behind.

Dancing in the dark as the ocean waves brushed her skin,
she felt the beauty of the breeze all around her and deep within.

All we have is the present and future, she thought.
So you may create a life anew at any time sought.
It's never too late to eat more healthy desserts,
and to play and laugh until it almost hurts.

We can find our footprints grazing the sand beneath our feet
in a land where new paths are always within our determined reach.

"To find your angels... Start trusting your inner voice and intuition." – Melanie Beckler

If I was going to create a devil's food cake, I had better create an angel's food cake too. Here is the result. I hope it brings a smile to your face as it did mine many times over.

ANGEL FOOD LAYER CAKE

MAKES
18 SERVINGS

PREHEAT
350°F

PREP TIME
NIGHT BEFORE &
15 MINUTES/LAYER

COOK TIME
40 MINUTES/LAYER

For the cake

½ cup non-dairy milk

16 medjool dates, pitted

2 tablespoons ground flaxseeds

½ cup cashew butter

1 ½ teaspoon vanilla bean powder

2 tablespoons lemon juice

2 teaspoons baking powder

1 cup almond flour

1 cup oat flour

For the coconut vanilla icing

8 medjool dates, pitted

¾ cup raw cashew butter or ½ cup raw cashews, soaked

3 cans coconut milk, refrigerated overnight, then liquid removed

1 ½ teaspoon vanilla bean powder

Night before: refrigerate coconut milk

Preheat oven to 350 degrees F.

Prepare in a 7-inch round springform pan with removable bottom. This cake can be made with one or two layers. If you are making a single layer cake, divide the ingredients in half. If you would like a double-layered cake, I recommend baking each layer separately in its own pan.

Process dates, flaxseeds, milk, cashew butter, vanilla, lemon juice and baking powder in a food processor. Blend until thoroughly mixed. Add almond flour and blend again for a few minutes. Lastly, add the oat flour and blend that in until a nice cake batter forms.

Using wet hands, shape the dough into a round ball. Flatten the dough in your cake pan, smoothing out the top.

Bake for 40 minutes or until a toothpick or fork inserted in the top comes out clean. Repeat for other layers to make a layered cake like my version in the photo.

To prepare the icing, process the pitted medjool dates with the cashew butter in your cleaned food processor until completely combined. Once it forms a smooth mixture, pour it into a small bowl and set aside.

Open the cans of refrigerated coconut milk and scoop out the hardened coconut mass, leaving the liquid behind. Place all icing ingredients, except for the vanilla powder, in a large bowl.

Whip all ingredients with an electric mixer, adding in the vanilla slowly until a nice vanilla icing is created. Spread the icing in between your cake layers and over the cake.

COCONUT CREAM TIRAMISU

MAKES
14 SERVINGS

METHOD
REFRIGERATE

PREP TIME
NIGHT BEFORE &
35 MINUTES

COOK TIME
NONE

---

10 ladyfinger cookies (page 16)

For the dipping sauce
1 cup freshly brewed coffee
2 tablespoons amaretto

For the coconut cream filling
8 medjool dates, pitted
½ cup raw cashew butter or
  ½ cup raw cashews, soaked
  overnight
2 tablespoons ground coffee
2 tablespoons amaretto
1 teaspoon vanilla bean powder
3 (15 oz.) cans coconut milk,
  refrigerated overnight, then
  liquid removed

Optional garnish
cacao powder
organic fresh berries

Night before: soak cashews, refrigerate coconut milk

Line a glass baking dish with parchment paper or tin foil. Place a large mixing bowl in the refrigerator to chill, for at least 10 minutes, to use for whipping the coconut cream.

Place all of the coconut cream filling ingredients, except for the two cans of refrigerated coconut milk, in a food processor and process until the mixture becomes completely smooth. Pour these ingredients out of the food processor and into a medium-sized bowl.

Use the two cans of refrigerated coconut milk to prepare coconut whipped cream. Make sure the coconut milk has been refrigerated overnight and the liquid removed from the can. Place the hardened coconut cream in your chilled mixing bowl and beat for 30 seconds with either an electric or one minute with a manual hand mixer. Stir the rest of the cream layer ingredients into the bowl with the whipped cream.

Combine the coffee and amaretto in a bowl and dip the ladyfinger cookies one by one into the mixture. Soak them each for about 30 seconds to 1 minute. Don't worry, they will not crumble or become overly mushy.

To assemble the tiramisu, layer half of the soaked ladyfinger cookies on the bottom of the prepared baking dish and add a nice layer of the whipped cream on top. Smooth down the whipped cream layer using a spatula or very large spoon. Place the remaining ladyfingers on top, creating a second layer. Follow with the rest of the coconut cream and then place the dish in the refrigerator overnight.

The next day, garnish with your favorite toppings such as cacao powder, shredded coconut and/or fresh berries and cut up into square slices.

Tiramisu originated in Italy in the 1960s. The word tiramisu translates to "pick me up," "cheer me up," "wake me up" or "lift me up."

I used a 9" heart-shaped pan with removable bottom, but you can use a round 6" springform pan. The key is to use a pan with a removable bottom. This will help enormously in mess prevention. The heart-shaped pan is fun and makes for one beautiful heart, but is not necessary.

To achieve the swirls you see on top use a sharp knife. Every single one of these cakes will have their own charm and unique beauty.

DARK CHOCOLATE JEWEL CAKE

MAKES
12 SERVINGS

METHOD
FREEZE

PREP TIME
NIGHT BEFORE &
30 MINUTES

COOK TIME
NONE

For the bottom walnut chocolate crust

⅓ cup almond milk

1 cup dried mulberries (soaked overnight in almond milk)

8 medjool dates, pitted

½ cup raw walnuts

½ cup cocoa powder

For the middle thin chocolate cream

8 medjool dates, pitted

½ cup cocoa powder

3 tablespoon raw cashew butter

2 tablespoons non-dairy milk

1 ½ teaspoon ground coffee (optional)

For the top creamy dark chocolate

¾ cup cocoa powder

1 15 oz. coconut milk, refrigerated overnight, then liquid removed*

8 medjool dates, pitted

1 ½ teaspoon vanilla bean powder

*After refrigeration overnight, the cream will have separated from the liquid. Drain the liquid and set aside, you will use only the cream for this recipe.

Night before: soak mulberries

The night before you make this recipe, soak dried mulberries in almond milk and refrigerate.

Pour off any remaining liquid used to soak the mulberries and save. Process all other crust ingredients in a food processor until all ingredients are evenly combined. You should get a sticky crumble. Transfer the sticky mixture into a springform pan and press into an even crust. Freeze it while you work on the middle layer.

Prepare the thinner middle layer. Add the dates to your cleaned food processor along with the cocoa powder, cashew butter, non-dairy milk, remaining mulberry soaking liquid, and coffee, if using. Process for a minute or so or until the mixture is completely smooth and creamy.

Take the bottom layer out of the freezer and spread this layer on it. Place back in the freezer while you prepare the top layer.

To prepare the top dark chocolate layer, simply process all of the ingredients in your cleaned food processor as you did with the bottom and middle layer. Once completely blended, take the pan out of the freezer and pour the chocolate layer on top of the pressed and flattened middle layer until it fills up the cake pan. If you desire, create decorative swirls on top using a sharp knife. Freeze the cake for 6 hours or overnight to set. Top with your favorite toppings after freezing. Keep leftovers frozen.

STRAWBERRY ICE CREAM CAKE

MAKES
18 SERVINGS

METHOD
FREEZE

PREP TIME
NIGHT BEFORE &
20 MINUTES

COOK TIME
NONE

For the chocolate crust

1 cup raw walnuts

1 cup cocoa powder

1 (15 oz.) can black beans

¾ cup almond milk (or non-dairy milk of choice)

22 medjool dates, pitted (divided into two piles)

For the middle coconut vanilla layer

1 (15 oz.) can coconut milk, refrigerated overnight, then liquid removed*

¼ cup raw cashew butter

2 very ripe, medium-sized bananas

12 medjool dates, pitted

1½ teaspoon vanilla bean powder

For the strawberry top layer

1 (10 oz.) bag organic frozen strawberries

1 (15 oz.) can coconut milk, refrigerated overnight, then liquid removed*

12 medjool dates, pitted

*After refrigeration overnight, the cream will have separated from the liquid. Drain the liquid and set aside, you will use only the cream for this recipe.

Night before: refrigerate coconut milk

This recipe calls for a round springform pan. I used a 9-inch pan with a removable bottom. Once you have your pan ready, you are ready to begin preparing the bottom layer.

In a food processor, grind up the raw walnuts until you have relatively fine walnut pieces. Add all other ingredients except for dates and combine. Add in 11 dates and process. Once the mixture is blended, add in the last batch of dates.

Once all ingredients have been added, process for another minute or so. Now you will have a smooth and creamy chocolaty crust. Pour this layer into the pan, smoothing out the top with a large spoon. Place this layer in the freezer as you begin preparing the coconut vanilla layer.

For the middle layer, blend all ingredients in a cleaned food processor and pour on top of the chocolate base layer. Smooth the top with your spoon and place the pan in the freezer once again as you prepare the top layer.

To prepare the top strawberry layer, process all of the ingredients in your cleaned food processor and pour the mixture on top of the middle layer, smoothing the top. Freeze again for at least 30 minutes.

Once the top layer is done freezing, add your favorite decorative toppings such as berries, grapes, figs, or chopped nuts.

If you blend all of the dates at once, the food processor may get jammed. A good trick when using a lot of dates is to divide them and add them to the food processor in two batches.

CHOCOLATE COFFEE CAKE

MAKES
10 SERVINGS

PREHEAT
350°F

PREP TIME
20 MINUTES

COOK TIME
20-25 MINUTES

For the chocolate cake

1 cup cocoa powder

1 (15 oz.) can black beans

10 medjool dates, pitted

½ cup oat flour

1 teaspoon baking powder

1 teaspoon baking soda

⅓ cup natural peanut butter

¼ cup water

1 tablespoon coffee

1 teaspoon cinnamon

For the icing

12 medjool dates, pitted

½ cup almond milk

½ cup cacao powder

1 teaspoon vanilla bean powder

Preheat oven to 350 degrees F.

Lightly grease a round springform cake pan with removable bottom (I used a 10-inch pan).

In a food processor, process all of the cake ingredients together except the cocoa powder. Once all ingredients are processed, then add cocoa powder and again process until all ingredients are combined.

Pour the batter into the springform pan and smooth out the top with the back of a large spoon.

Bake for 20-25 minutes and take out of the oven and let cool for at least 15 minutes.

Prepare the chocolate icing while the cake is baking. Combine all of the icing ingredients in a food processor or high-powered blender until smooth and creamy. Once the cake is done baking and has cooled, pour the chocolaty icing on top and smooth it over the cake evenly.

Garnish with some fresh berries if you'd like.

NUT-FREE CHOCOLATE CAKE

MAKES
12 SERVINGS

METHOD
FREEZE

PREP TIME
15 MINUTES

COOK TIME
NONE

For the chocolate cake

2 cups white mulberries, ground

12 medjool dates, pitted

¾ cup cocoa powder

1 tablespoon non-dairy milk

1 tablespoon lemon juice

1 ½ teaspoon vanilla bean powder

3 tablespoons coconut butter

For the icing

½ cup coconut butter, softened

⅓ cup cocoa powder

¼ cup non-dairy milk of choice

1 ripe banana

4 medjool dates, pitted

Toppings (optional)

cocoa nibs

shredded coconut

dried rose petals

dried lavender

For this recipe you will need a 6-inch springform pan lined with parchment paper.

Process all cake ingredients in a food processor until everything is thoroughly combined. Mold the dough into a firm ball and transfer to pan.

Press the cake firmly into the pan using a large spoon and then by placing a piece of parchment paper on top and pressing down on the cake to achieve a flat, even and smooth surface. Once the surface is smooth, place the cake in the freezer while you prepare the icing.

To prepare the icing, place all of the ingredients in your cleaned food processor or a high-powered blender and blend until the icing is smooth and creamy. Remove the cake from the freezer and pour the chocolate icing over the cake using a large spoon or spatula to spread the icing evenly and smoothly over the top.

Decorate as you wish with any topping of your liking. If you decide to use fresh berries or other fruit, add them after the cake freezes directly before serving. Place the cake in your freezer for at least 3 hours to set and chill.

Defrost individual slices by leaving out for 30 minutes.

Dried mulberries are a fantastic alternative to other sweeteners or nuts in raw cakes. If you prepare this cake for yourself, slice it into 10 individual pieces and freeze each piece in tin foil. You can take a slice out of the freezer at your leisure whenever a chocolaty craving strikes.

For this recipe, I recommend a pan with a removable bottom. I used a 6" round springform pan. You can use a round, heart-shaped, or rectangular pan with this recipe. The removable bottom is key so that the cake is easier to remove from the pan.

An alternative to soaking the pineapple overnight is soaking it in water and heating in the microwave for 30 seconds. This will soften the dried pineapple before adding it to the food processor.

To soften dates, you can soak them in water overnight or soak them in water and heat them in the microwave for 30 seconds before using your electric mixer to beat them in.

PINEAPPLE CARROT CAKE

MAKES
16 SERVINGS

PREHEAT
350ºF

PREP TIME
NIGHT BEFORE &
20 MINUTES

COOK TIME
40-50 MINUTES/LAYER

For the carrot cake

3 flax "eggs"
(3 tablespoons ground
flaxseeds + ½ cup
non-dairy milk)

1 cup unsweetened applesauce

8 medjool dates, pitted

6 slices dried pineapple (¾ cup
loosely packed), soaked in
water overnight

⅓ cup coconut butter or vegan
butter, melted

1 tablespoon apple cider vinegar

2 teaspoons baking powder

2 teaspoons cinnamon

1 teaspoon nutmeg

1½ teaspoon vanilla bean
powder

1½ cup almond flour

1½ cup oat flour

1½ cup grated carrot

½ cup organic raisins

½ cup walnuts

For the lemon vanilla icing:

2 (15 oz) cans coconut
milk, refrigerated overnight, then
liquid removed*

8 medjool dates, pitted

2 teaspoons vanilla bean powder

2 tablespoons lemon juice

*After refrigeration overnight, the
cream will have separated from
the liquid. Drain the liquid and set
aside, you will use only the cream
for this recipe.

Night before: soak pineapple, refrigerate coconut milk

Preheat oven to 350 degrees F.

Lightly grease two 6-inch round springform pans with removable bottom with coconut oil or cooking spray. For the icing, refrigerate a large mixing bowl for a least ten minutes.

Mix ground flaxseeds with non-dairy milk in a cup or small bowl. Stir and let sit for a minute to create flax "eggs."

Add flax "eggs" to a food processor along with all carrot cake ingredients except the flours. Process for a minute or until smooth. Then add almond flour and process that into the mixture as well. Pour this mixture into a large mixing bowl. Add oat flour and stir. Stir in grated carrot, raisins, and walnuts too. The batter should be thick, but pourable. If too thick, add a few tablespoons of non-dairy milk. Divide evenly among cake pans.

Bake for 40-50 minutes or until deep golden brown and a toothpick inserted into the center comes out clean. Note that the size of pan you use will vary baking time.

Remove from oven and let rest in the pans for 15 minutes. Then carefully run a knife along the edges and gently invert onto cooling racks to let cool completely. This cake benefits from cooling completely before icing. If short on time, you can speed the cooling by placing the cakes in the refrigerator or freezer until very cool to the touch.

To prepare icing, remove coconut milk from the refrigerator and remove the liquid from the can. Place the hardened coconut cream in a chilled mixing bowl and beat for 30 seconds with an electric or one minute with a hand mixer. I recommend using an electric mixer because it is much easier. Stir the rest of the icing ingredients into the bowl. The icing should be fluffy and the texture quite a bit like real whipped cream. Ice the cake and decorate to your liking.

The chocolate non-dairy milk can be homemade or purchased. I even like to substitute the non-dairy milk with a non-dairy mocha.

You can use pumpkin (or sweet potato) from a can for this recipe, but I like to bake/roast mine and then mash it because the flavors are richer this way.

The coconut water that remains from the coconut milk can be used for any recipe calling for non-dairy milk, so you don't have to throw it out.

PUMPKIN BUTTER LAYER CAKE

MAKES
14 SERVINGS

METHOD
FREEZE

PREP TIME
NIGHT BEFORE &
12 MINUTES

COOK TIME
NONE

For the chocolate cake

1 cup mulberries, ground

10 medjool dates, pitted

½ cup non-dairy chocolate milk

1 tablespoon almond extract

3 tablespoons peanut butter

2 tablespoons ground flaxseeds

⅓ cup cocoa powder

½ cup almond flour

1 cup oat flour

2 teaspoons baking powder

1 tablespoon coconut butter

For the peanut butter pumpkin cream

2 (15 oz.) cans coconut milk, refrigerated overnight, then liquid removed* (to make coconut whipped cream)

3 tablespoons peanut butter

½ cup pumpkin, mashed

9 medjool dates, pitted and softened

1 ripe banana

2 teaspoons vanilla bean powder

*After refrigeration overnight, the cream will have separated from the liquid. Drain the liquid and set aside, you will use only the cream for this recipe.

Night before: refrigerate coconut milk

For this recipe, you will need a 6-inch round springform pan. Line the pan with parchment paper.

Process the ground mulberries and dates with non-dairy milk or chocolate non-dairy milk. Add peanut butter and ground flaxseeds to the food processor and process well before finally adding the cocoa powder and almond flour. When smooth, pour it into a large mixing bowl and stir in the oat flour, using your hands to make the dough.

Melt coconut butter by heating in the microwave for 30 seconds and stirring. It may need an additional 30 seconds to completely melt. Add melted coconut butter to make the dough workable to be molded into a cake. Move cake dough to pan and flatten evenly. Place the pan containing the cake in the freezer while you prepare the pumpkin peanut butter coconut cream icing.

Make coconut whipped cream by scooping out the hardened coconut mass from the two cans of refrigerated coconut milk leaving any liquid behind. Use an electric or manual hand mixer and beat the coconut mass until a smooth cream forms. Place the other icing ingredients in your cleaned food processor and process thoroughly. Pour the mixture into the bowl with the coconut whipped cream and whip together.

Take the cake out of the freezer and using a large, sharp knife, cut the cake into three horizontal, even layers (see picture). Smooth out some of the peanut butter pumpkin cream icing on top of layer of cake. Place the iced-up layer back in the freezer for about 30 minutes (on a small cutting board or plate), so that the pumpkin cream can harden over the cake. Once frozen, place a layer of the chocolate cake on top and smooth icing over top.

Place the cake back in the freezer for another 30 minutes so that the cream layer can harden before finally adding another layer of chocolate cake. Once you've placed the last layer of chocolate cake on top of the cream, place the cake back in the freezer so that the final chocolate layer can firm up. After freezing for another 30 minutes, you can spread the remaining peanut butter pumpkin cream all over the outside of the cake (as photographed).

Decorate with cacao powder sprinkled on top, perhaps a flower (or two or three).

PEANUT BUTTER PIE

MAKES
15 SERVINGS

PREHEAT
350°F

PREP TIME
35 MINUTES

COOK TIME
20 MINUTES

For the chocolate crust

¼ cup cocoa powder

½ cup raw walnuts (or other nuts)

½ cup shredded unsweetened coconut

10 medjool dates, pitted

For the ultra-peanut butter filling

2 teaspoons agar agar powder

2 tablespoons of water

1 cup peanut butter

¾ cup date sugar*

2 ripe bananas

1 teaspoon vanilla bean powder

Optional toppings

2 ounces melted vegan dark chocolate

coconut whipped cream

dark chocolate shavings

*__Note:__ Date sugar is simply ground up dates. You can find it in many health food stores and online

Preheat oven to 350 degrees F.

To prepare the crust, process cocoa powder, walnuts and shredded coconut in a food processor for a few minutes until all ingredients have been combined. Then add dates and process until the dates have been completely mixed in.

Mold the crust around the rims of your pans evenly. Place the crusted molds in the fridge while you prepare the filling.

To prepare the peanut butter filling, mix and dissolve the agar agar powder into 2 tablespoons of water. Add the agar agar mix and all of the ingredients except for the unsweetened baking chocolate to the food processor and process for a few minutes until all ingredients have been thoroughly combined.

Take the crusted molds out of refrigerator and using a big spoon, pour the peanut butter filling into each one, smoothing out the top.

For optional topping, melt the chocolate by heating in the microwave for 30 seconds in a small bowl. Using a small spoon, use melted dark chocolate to decorate the tops of each cake.

Refrigerate for at least 30 minutes, then bake for 20 minutes. Top with your favorite toppings such as fresh berries and edible flowers.

For this recipe, I used three 6x6 inch pans with removable bottoms, but you can use one or two larger pans.

PISTACHIO CREAM CAKE

MAKES
20 SERVINGS

METHOD
FREEZE

PREP TIME
NIGHT BEFORE &
12 MINUTES

COOK TIME
NONE

For the pistachio base layer

1 cup raw Mediterranean pine nuts, soaked in water overnight (walnuts, pecans or almonds also works)

1 cup raw pistachio nuts, soaked in water overnight

12 medjool dates, pitted

1 teaspoon vanilla bean powder

For the middle vanilla layer

1 (15 oz.) can coconut milk, refrigerated overnight, then liquid removed*

⅓ cup coconut butter

1 cup canned white beans

10 medjool dates, pitted

1 tablespoon vanilla bean powder

For the top chocolate layer

1 (15 oz.) can coconut milk, refrigerated overnight, then liquid removed*

1 cup raw cashew butter

1 cup cocoa powder

1 ripe banana

8 medjool dates, pitted

*After refrigeration overnight, the cream will have separated from the liquid. Drain the liquid and set aside, you will use only the cream for this recipe.

Night before: soak pine nuts, pistachio nuts, refrigerate coconut milk

Blend all base layer ingredients in a food processor until evenly mixed. Spread the mixture in a cake pan of choice. I used a 9-inch pan with removable bottom.

Flatten base layer completely using a large spoon or your hands. Place in the freezer for 10 minutes so it hardens a bit while you prepare the middle layer.

To prepare the middle vanilla layer, simply place all ingredients in your cleaned food processor and process until thoroughly mixed. When you add the chilled coconut milk from the can to the food processor, make sure to add only the coconut cream and not the coconut liquid.

Spread and flatten the vanilla layer on top of the bottom pistachio layer. Place back in the freezer while you prepare the top layer.

Process the top layer in your cleaned food processor until smooth and creamy. Again, make sure not to add any coconut liquid from the coconut milk can, just the coconut cream.

Spread the chocolaty top layer evenly on top of the middle layer. Place back in the freezer for at least an hour so the entire cake can firm up. Slice and serve.

HALF-BAKED STRAWBERRY CAKE

MAKES
16 SERVINGS

PREHEAT
350°F

PREP TIME
NIGHT BEFORE &
25 MINUTES

COOK TIME
25 MINUTES

For the dark chocolate bottom layer

3 flax "eggs"
(3 tablespoons ground flaxseeds + ½ cup non-dairy milk)

1 cup cacao powder

1 cup oat flour

½ cup almond flour

12 medjool dates, pitted

1 ½ teaspoons baking powder

For the top strawberry layer

2 cups frozen organic strawberries, defrosted

2 (15 oz) cans coconut milk, refrigerated overnight, then liquid removed

½ cup coconut butter

15 medjool dates, pitted

½ Pitaya Plus smoothie pack (for extra pink color)

*After refrigeration overnight, the cream will have separated from the liquid. Drain the liquid and set aside, you will use only the cream for this recipe.

Night before: refrigerate coconut milk

Preheat oven to 350 degrees F.

Lightly grease a round 8x8 inch springform cake pan with removable bottom.

Prepare the bottom chocolate layer first. The bottom layer is baked and the top layer isn't. Combine ground flaxseeds with non-dairy milk in a small bowl or cup and stir. Let sit for a minute so a nice gel forms to make your "eggs."

Place the flax "eggs" and all other chocolate layer ingredients in a food processor and process until thoroughly mixed. It will be a bit crumbly but should mold well into a firm crust. Add a bit of water if necessary.

Flatten out the crust in the prepared pan, making sure you flatten the top so it is nice and even. Using a pan with a removable bottom is key.

Bake for 25 minutes while you prepare the top strawberry layer.

To prepare the strawberry top layer, add defrosted strawberries to a cleaned food processor (make sure not to add any liquid that results from defrosting) along with the rest of the ingredients and process until completely combined.

Once the bottom layer is done baking, take it out of the oven, allow it to cool and place it in the freezer for just ten minutes so it can cool a bit more.

Pour the strawberry layer on top, flattening the top with a large spoon and then place in the freezer for at least an hour before decorating/cutting into slices.

Decorate with your favorite toppings.

BERRY MANGO RAINBOW CAKE

MAKES
10 SERVINGS

METHOD
FREEZE

PREP TIME
NIGHT BEFORE &
25 MINUTES

COOK TIME
NONE

For the crust

1 cup mulberries, ground and soaked in ¼ cup non-dairy milk overnight

4 medjool dates, pitted

½ cup raw walnuts

¼ cup shredded coconut

For the middle mango layer

1 (15 oz.) can coconut milk, refrigerated overnight, then liquid removed*

½ cup fresh or frozen mango, defrosted

5 medjool dates, pitted

1½ teaspoon vanilla bean powder

For the top raspberry layer

1 (15 oz.) can coconut milk, refrigerated overnight, then liquid removed*

1 cup raspberries

5 medjool dates, pitted

1½ teaspoon vanilla bean powder

Optional toppings

fresh berries

shredded coconut

shaved chocolate

edible flowers

*After refrigeration overnight, the cream will have separated from the liquid. Drain the liquid and set aside, you will use only the cream for this recipe.

Night before: soak mulberries, refrigerate coconut milk

Process all crust ingredients in a food processor to a sticky crumble. Transfer the sticky mixture into the springform pan and press into an even crust. Freeze it while you work on the middle layer.

Blend all middle layer ingredients in your cleaned food processor until a smooth, uniform mixture forms.

Take the pan out of the freezer and pour this layer on top. Smooth it out evenly with a large spoon.

Place the cake back in the freezer while you prepare the top raspberry layer.

Process the top raspberry layer ingredients in your cleaned food processor and pour on top of the mango layer.

Create decorative swirls on top using a knife. Freeze the cake for 6 hours or overnight to set. Top with your favorite toppings after freezing.

Freeze leftovers.

I used a 9" heart-shaped pan with removable bottom, but you can use a round 6" spring form pan. The key is to use a pan with a removable bottom. This will help enormously in preventing a mess.

FALL SPICE CAKE

MAKES
12 SERVINGS

PREHEAT
365°F

PREP TIME
20 MINUTES

COOK TIME
40 MINUTES

For the food processor

12 medjool dates, pitted

½ cup of non-dairy milk of choice

3 tablespoons ground flaxseeds mixed with non-dairy milk of choice

½ cup canned white beans, liquid removed

2 ripe large bananas

1 ½ teaspoon vanilla bean powder

2 teaspoons baking powder

1 teaspoon ground cinnamon

1 teaspoon ground nutmeg

½ teaspoon ground cloves

½ teaspoon ground ginger

¼ cup rum (optional)

For the dry ingredients

1 cup spelt flour

1 cup oat flour

For the dough

3 cups apples, cored and chopped

½ cup organic raisins

½ cup chopped hazelnuts

Preheat oven to 365 degrees F.

Lightly grease a 10-inch round springform pan, preferably with a removable bottom and line with parchment paper.

Process all food processor ingredients in a food processor until thoroughly mixed, adding the baking powder and spices at this time.

Mix the processed ingredients with dry ingredients in a large bowl until a nice cake dough forms.

Stir in chopped apples, raisins and hazelnuts evenly into the dough. Flatten the dough evenly in the pan.

Bake for 40 minutes. Once finished baking, allow it to cool for at least 15 minutes before slicing.

There are two major types of cinnamon used in food preparation in America:

CEYLON CINNAMON
Native to Sri Lanka, it is also known as "true cinnamon." It is not the predominant spice typically sold as cinnamon in the United States. Ceylon is considered a finer quality spice due to its sweeter, more delicate and complex flavor.

CASSIA CINNAMON
This type is the most commonly used in America and is the type most commonly found in grocery stores. It's native to Burma and grown in China and Vietnam. Less expensive and slightly darker in color compared to Ceylon, it has a stronger, more pungent flavor. The critical difference: The coumarin content of cassia cinnamon is enough to potentially be toxic. Coumarin is a naturally occurring toxin that has the potential to damage the liver in high doses. Cassia contains high levels of coumarin, whereas Ceylon cinnamon contains either undetectable levels or only traces of coumarin.[1,2]

Both types are derived from the inner bark of Cinnamomum trees and cinnamon promotes healthy blood glucose levels, so use mostly Ceylon cinnamon if you love cinnamon.

GINGERBREAD LAYER CAKE

MAKES
22 SERVINGS

PREHEAT
350°F

PREP TIME
NIGHT BEFORE &
35 MINUTES

COOK TIME
40 MINUTES

2 flax "eggs"
(2 tablespoons ground
flaxseeds + ½ cup
non-dairy milk)

12 medjool dates, pitted

1 ripe banana

1 can (15 oz.) white beans,
drained of liquid

1½ teaspoon vanilla bean
powder

1 teaspoon cinnamon

½ teaspoon nutmeg

½ teaspoon ground ginger

2 teaspoons baking powder

1 cup raw cashew butter

½ cup almond flour

1½ cups oat flour

1¼ cup grated apple, loosely
packed (about 3 apples)

For the cashew cream frosting

¾ cup raw cashews soaked
overnight or heated for 15
minutes in boiling water

1 cup coconut butter

8 medjool dates, pitted

1 ripe banana

⅓ cup non-dairy milk

½ teaspoon vanilla bean powder

Night before: soak cashews

Preheat oven to 350 F. Lightly grease two 7- or 8-inch springform cake pans with removable bottoms.

In a cup or small bowl, mix ground flaxseeds with non-dairy milk, stir and let sit for a minute to form flax "eggs." Add flax "eggs" and pitted dates to a food processor along with the banana, beans, vanilla, cinnamon, nutmeg, ground ginger and baking powder. Thoroughly process then add cashew butter, almond flour and 1 cup of the oat flour. Process again for another minute or so until all ingredients are combined. Lastly, add remaining cup of oat flour and process until a smooth dough forms. Pour the dough into a large mixing bowl and stir in grated apple pieces. Evenly distribute the dough between both pans, smoothing the top of each one. It may look like there's not enough batter but there is. It will rise while baking.

Bake for about 40 minutes. You'll know it's done when a toothpick inserted into the center comes out clean and the edges should be slightly browned. Take out from the oven and set out on counter to cool completely.

While the cake is cooling, prepare the frosting. Add all frosting ingredients to your cleaned food processor and process until completely combined. The frosting will be somewhat thick and this is desirable because you don't want any frosting to slide off the cake. Once the cake is completely cooled, add ⅔ of the frosting to the top of each cake and spread it on evenly. Use the remaining ⅓ of the frosting to the sides. Add crushed nuts, cacao nibs, flowers or any other decorative toppings. Slice and serve.

To save time, you can place large apple chunks in the food processor and process instead of chopping or grating apples.

The cake should be covered if stored in the fridge for freshness and will last for 3-4 days if stored there. It will last for 3-4 weeks if stored in the freezer.

A reminder for health nuts about the relationship between nuts and longevity.

What's noteworthy about pistachios in particular is that they contain the highest plant sterol content of all nuts. Plant sterols (also called phytosterols) are the plant version of cholesterol. They help lower our cholesterol levels in a very interesting way.

Because plant sterols are structurally similar to human cholesterol, they bind to the sites on the cells lining the small intestine that human cholesterol would. This is one way that plant sterols block the absorption of cholesterol from food and the re-absorption of cholesterol produced by the liver. Over forty human trials have collectively demonstrated that plant sterol can safely reduce LDL levels by up to 15 percent.[3-5]

PISTACHIO CHOCOLATE CREAM PIE

MAKES
18 SERVINGS

METHOD
REFRIGERATE

PREP TIME
20 MINUTES

COOK TIME
NONE

For the crust

2 cups unsweetened shredded coconut or coconut flakes

1 ½ cup raw pistachios, unsalted

1 ½ cup raw pumpkin seeds, unsalted

12 medjool dates, pitted

1 cup cocoa powder

For the chocolate whipped cream filling

1 (15 oz.) can full fat coconut milk

1 cup canned black beans

¾ cup ultra dark cocoa powder

15 medjool dates, pitted

1 ½ teaspoon vanilla bean powder

Optional toppings

fresh fruit

For this recipe, you will need a 7-inch tart pan or dish of a similar size with a removable bottom.

Place all crust ingredients in a food processor and just process enough so that there are still plenty of nut/seed pieces, but coarse enough that you can mold into a nice crust.

Form the mixture into a pie crust in a pan by pressing it down with your hands until it's even all around the edges and the bottom is flat. Place the pan into the freezer to firm up while working on the filling.

Place all chocolate filling ingredients into the cleaned food processor. Pour mixture into the prepared pie crust and flatten the top. You can form a nice chocolate swirl on top using a large spoon. Place the pie in your freezer while you prepare the toppings.

Once the chocolate filling in the pie is firm (this should take about 10-15 minutes in the freezer), place optional fruit on top.

Place pie in the fridge and allow it to set about an hour. For a smooth consistency, let the pie sit at room temp for about 15-20 minutes before serving.

This pie can also be enjoyed right out of the fridge, although the chocolate filling will be firm.

CHOCOLATE CRUSTED CHERRY PIE

MAKES
24 SERVINGS

METHOD
REFRIGERATE

PREP TIME
NIGHT BEFORE &
30-35 MINUTES

COOK TIME
15 MINUTES

For the vanilla cashew crust

3 cups raw cashews (soaked in water overnight or boiled for 15 minutes)

20 medjool dates, pitted

3 tablespoons coconut butter, softened

2½ tablespoons ground vanilla (I used Tahitian vanilla)

For the chocolate almond crust

1 cup almond flour

10 medjool dates, pitted

½ cup cocoa powder

2 tablespoons vegan margarine or coconut butter, softened, for oil-free version

For the cherry filling

5½ cups pitted cherries

¾ cups date sugar*

⅓ cup arrowroot powder

½ teaspoon fresh lemon zest (optional)

*Note: Date sugar is simply ground up dates. You can find it in many health food stores and online.

Night before: soak cashews

Combine all of the vanilla cashew crust ingredients in a food processor and process until the ingredients are thoroughly combined. Place this layer in a large bowl and set aside.

Clean your food processor and do the same for the top chocolate almond crust layer. Pour into a large bowl and set aside.

If using a standard pie pan, roll the vanilla cashew dough into a ball and flatten it well in the pie dish. (I recommend molding the chocolate almond crust layer around the underlying cashew crust (see photos). If you want to get fancy, you can do what I did and prepare a special decorative edge around the outer rim of the crust.)

Place the crust in the freezer for 15-20 minutes to harden and begin preparing the cherry filling. Pit all cherries or allow frozen cherries to thaw and remove the liquid. Place into a large pan, and add date sugar, cornstarch and optional lemon zest. Cook on medium heat for about 5 minutes, stirring well.

Turn off heat, take crust out of the freezer and pour the filling on top of the now hardened vanilla chocolate crust. Cut into slices and enjoy chilled, warmed in the microwave for a minute or baked for 15 minutes.

If doing the oil-free version with coconut butter, soften coconut butter in the microwave by heating for 30 seconds. Then it will process better with the rest of the ingredients.

You can prepare this flourless cherry pie in a standard pie dish, a 9-inch springform cake pan or even a square 9x9 inch cake pan. I prepared this in my favorite heart-shaped cake pan with removable bottom. If you use a smaller pan, you can turn the extra dough into cookies.

RAW ICE CREAM CAKE

MAKES
18 SERVINGS

METHOD
REFRIGERATE

PREP TIME
NIGHT BEFORE &
25-30 MINUTES

COOK TIME
NONE

For the chocolate crust

1 cup almond flour

8 medjool dates, pitted

½ cup cocoa powder

2 tablespoons coconut butter

For the middle vanilla layer

1½ cups combination of cashew &
macadamia nuts, soaked in water
overnight then drained

½ of 15 oz. can full fat coconut
milk, refrigerated overnight, then
liquid removed*

8 medjool dates, pitted and
softened

5 tablespoons lemon juice

1 tablespoon vanilla bean powder

For the strawberry top layer

1½ cups combination of cashew &
macadamia nuts, soaked in water
overnight then drained

½ of 15 oz. can full fat coconut
milk, refrigerated overnight, then
liquid removed*

8 medjool dates, pitted and
softened

5 tablespoons lemon juice (juice of
1 large lemon)

1 tablespoon vanilla bean powder

1 cup fresh or frozen organic
strawberries

Optional toppings

Fresh berries or shredded coconut

*After refrigeration overnight, the
cream will have separated from
the liquid. Drain the liquid and set
aside, you will use only the cream
for this recipe.

Night before: soak cashews, macadamia nuts, refrigerate coconut
milk

Place ground almonds, pitted dates, cocoa powder in a food
processor and blend until crumbly. Add coconut butter and process
some more until the mixture is well combined and sticks together
when squeezed between your fingers.

Press the chocolaty crust mixture into the bottom of a 6-inch
springform pan using your fingers or the back of a tablespoon. If
making a larger cake is desired you can use a larger springform
pan and double the crust ingredient amounts, simply repeating this
process. (I prepared this cake in a heart-shaped pan, but you don't
have to.)

Set aside while you prepare the middle vanilla layer.

Clean the food processor and blend all of the middle layer
ingredients until the mixture is creamy and smooth. Make sure not
to add any liquid from the coconut can, only the coconut cream.

Pour this mixture on top of the chocolaty layer and smooth the
top with a large spoon so that the top of this layer is completely
smooth. Place in the freezer to harden for 15 minutes while you
prepare the strawberry layer.

To prepare the strawberry layer, do just as you did to prepare the
vanilla layer, but add the strawberries this time around. After the
middle vanilla layer has hardened, take it out of the freezer and
gently pour the strawberry layer on top, smoothing the top of this
layer so that it is even.

Freeze for another 15 minutes before placing your favorite
toppings on the top of the cake.

Blueberries contain a type of antioxidant called tannins and plenty of unique flavonoids too, all crossing our blood-brain barriers and exerting tangible improvements in existing neural pathways, cellular communication, and neural regeneration and strengthening. While blueberries have been shown to significantly reduce our odds of age-related mental decline, memory loss, dementia, and Alzheimer's in later years, research on humans also shows that consuming blueberries improves learning and word recall in the present, as well as a reduction in depressive symptoms.[6,7]

VANILLA BLUEBERRY CHEESECAKE

MAKES
18 SERVINGS

METHOD
REFRIGERATE

PREP TIME
NIGHT BEFORE &
25-30 MINUTES

COOK TIME
NONE

For the crust

1 cup cashews, soaked overnight

½ cup almonds

1 cup shredded coconut

1 cup medjool dates, pitted

1 tablespoon vanilla bean powder

2 tablespoons water

For the chocolate layer (optional)

8 medjool dates, pitted

½ cup cocoa powder

1 cup raw walnuts or hemp seeds

1 cup raw cashew butter

1 tablespoon mesquite powder
(optional)

For the blueberry cheesecake

1 (15 oz.) can coconut milk,
refrigerated overnight, then
liquid removed*

1 cup shredded coconut

½ cup white beans, canned

10 medjool dates, pitted and
blended with ⅓ cup water

2 cups fresh or frozen blueberries

1½ teaspoon vanilla bean powder

For the blueberry jam

2 tablespoons ground chia seeds

2 tablespoons coconut water or
regular water

1 cups frozen blueberries, thawed

6 medjool dates blended with ⅓
cup water

1 teaspoon vanilla bean powder

*After refrigeration overnight, the
cream will have separated from
the liquid. Drain the liquid and set
aside, you will use only the cream
for this recipe.

Night before: soak cashews, refrigerate coconut milk

In a food processor, process the cashews, almonds and coconut into fine pieces. Add dates, vanilla and water and process until completely combined. Press crust evenly into a 9-inch round springform pan, pressing the top of the crust down firmly and evenly. Freeze the crust for at least 15 minutes.

(optional) To prepare the chocolate middle layer, process all ingredients in your food processor until smooth and creamy. Spread this layer on the cashew crust and place back in the freezer.

To prepare the jam, stir the chia seeds in with water in a small bowl or cup and set in the fridge for 10 minutes while the seeds form a nice gel. Then use a blender or food processor to blend the blueberries, dates and vanilla. Pour this mixture into a small bowl and place it back in the fridge while you prepare the cheesecake.

Process all the blueberry cheesecake ingredients in your food processor. Make sure to only use the solid coconut portion and not the coconut liquid from the can of coconut milk.

Take the crust out of the freezer and pour the cheesecake evenly over it. Don't worry if the cheesecake is a bit too liquid. It will firm up once you place it in the freezer.

Place the cheesecake in the freezer for at least one hour so it can solidify. Once it's done solidifying, place as much jam and other toppings on top of the cake as you desire.

Note: You might have quite a bit of jam left over.

The cheesecake will last for about three weeks if stored in the freezer and about five days if stored in the fridge.

TROPICAL CREAM PIE

MAKES
14 SERVINGS

METHOD
REFRIGERATE

PREP TIME
NIGHT BEFORE &
18 MINUTES

COOK TIME
NONE

For the crust

1 cup cashews, soaked overnight

½ cup macadamia nuts

1 cup shredded coconut

10 medjool dates, pitted

1 ½ teaspoon vanilla bean powder

2 tablespoons non-dairy milk or water

For the tropical mango topping

1 (15 oz.) can full fat coconut milk, refrigerated overnight, then liquid removed*

1 ½ cup fresh or frozen mango, defrosted

½ cup freeze dried or dried pineapple

1 large ripe banana

½ cup cooked or canned white beans

8 medjool dates, pitted and softened

*After refrigeration overnight, the cream will have separated from the liquid. Drain the liquid and set aside, you will use only the cream for this recipe.

Night before: soak cashews, refrigerate coconut milk

Process the cashew crust ingredients in a food processor, and mold into a large ball. Flatten it out evenly in a 9-inch round springform pan with removable bottom. Then place in the freezer for 30 minutes.

Combine the mango topping ingredients in a cleaned food processor until smooth. Then pour on top of the cashew crust, smoothing with a large spoon.

Place the pie back in the freezer for at least 30 minutes to firm up.

Once the pie has solidified, take it out of the freezer and out of the round springform pan. Top with your favorite toppings, such as shredded coconut, fresh or defrosted frozen fruit and/or coconut whipped cream.

CHOCOLATE AVO TORTE

MAKES
9 SERVINGS

METHOD
FREEZE

PREP TIME
20 MINUTES

COOK TIME
NONE

For the oat crust

1 very ripe large banana, peeled

½ cup cooked or canned white beans

5 medjool dates, pitted

½ cup rolled or old-fashioned oats

⅓ cup sunflower seeds

2 tablespoons ground flaxseeds

1½ teaspoon vanilla bean powder

For the chocolate avocado mousse filling

1 ripe avocado, pitted

5 medjool dates, pitted

½ cup cocoa powder

½ cup black beans (white also works)

1 teaspoon vanilla bean powder

For the toppings

fresh berries

kiwis

bananas

mulberries

Place crust ingredients in a food processor and process until smooth. Mold the crust into three, 3-inch diameter round torte pans or one large pie pan. It is helpful if the pans have removable bottoms.

Once the oat crust has been molded into the pan(s), place them into the freezer for at least 15 minutes while you prepare the chocolate avocado mousse filling.

Process all mousse ingredients until smooth and creamy. You might need to add a few tablespoons water or non-dairy milk so that all ingredients are well blended.

Remove the crust from the freezer and pour the mousse filling into each pan.

Top with your favorite fruit toppings.

RASPBERRY LOVIN' TORTE

MAKES
10 SERVINGS

PREHEAT
350°F

PREP TIME
NIGHT BEFORE &
25 MINUTES

COOK TIME
40 MINUTES

For the almond crust

1 ½ cups almond flour

½ cup oat flour

⅓ cup white beans

2 tablespoons coconut butter

10 medjool dates, pitted

For the raspberry filling

1 (15 oz) can coconut milk,
  refrigerated overnight, then
  liquid removed*

⅓ cup nondairy yogurt of choice

5 medjool dates, pitted

2 tablespoons coconut butter or
  raw cashew butter

1 cup organic fresh or frozen
  raspberries

*After refrigeration overnight, the
cream will have separated from
the liquid. Drain the liquid and
set aside, you will use only the
cream for this recipe.

Night before: refrigerate coconut milk

Preheat oven to 350 degrees F.

Mix all almond crust ingredients (except for oat flour) in a food
processor until evenly combined. Then add oat flour and process
that in evenly. With the processed almond crust mixture, create one
large dough ball and put it in tin foil and freeze for at least a half
hour so it can firm up.

After the dough ball has firmed up a bit, mold it into a springform
cake pan with a removable bottom (I used a heart shaped one as
you can see). I recommend a pan of about 9-inch diameter. Spread
dough evenly along the pan with your fingers. I made a nice design
as you can see in the photo. After spreading the dough again freeze
for 10 minutes before baking for 40 minutes or until the torte has
a slightly golden crust and is firm on the inside. Allow the baked
crust to cool down before you pour in the filling.

To prepare the filling, blend all raspberry filling ingredients in a
food processor or high-powered blender until smooth and creamy.
Make sure to add only the coconut cream from the can and not
the liquid portion too. Pour the filling over the cooled crust and
smooth the top so that it is nice and even.

Refrigerate the prepared torte for at least one hour before slicing
and top with your favorite fresh fruit.

Raspberries contain many health-promoting phytonutrients that possess antioxidant, antimicrobial,
and anticarcinogenic properties. Raspberries contain ellagitannins, a family of compounds almost
exclusive to the raspberry that have been shown to possess anti-cancer properties as well as
anthocynanins, ellagic acid, catechins, and other flavonoids. The ellagic acid content of raspberries
helps prevent damage to our cell membranes and other structures in the body by defending us
from free-radical damage. Given that free-radical damage is a large component of what ages us,
raspberries are an anti-aging food.[8-13]

WALNUT RUM MOCHA CAKE

MAKES
16 SERVINGS

PREHEAT
350°F

PREP TIME
NIGHT BEFORE &
20 MINUTES

COOK TIME
45 MINUTES

For the cake

¾ cup cacao powder

2 teaspoons baking powder

16 medjool dates, pitted

⅓ cup raw cashew butter

1 cup non-dairy milk of choice

¼ cup rum

1½ teaspoon vanilla bean powder

1 tablespoon ground coffee of choice, optional

½ cup walnut flour

1½ cups spelt flour (or ½ cup almond flour + 1 cup oat flour for gluten-free version)

¼ cup raw walnut pieces, optional

For the icing

3 (15 oz) cans coconut milk, refrigerated overnight, then liquid removed*

4 tablespoons cacao powder

6 medjool dates, pitted

For the topping

crushed walnuts

shaved chocolate

pomegranate seeds

*After refrigeration overnight, the cream will have separated from the liquid. Drain the liquid and set aside, you will use only the cream for this recipe.

Night before: refrigerate coconut milk

Preheat oven to 350 degrees F.

For the icing, chill a mixing bowl for 10 minutes.

To prepare the cake, simply add all of the cake ingredients, except flours and walnut pieces, to your clean food processor. Once all ingredients are processed, add walnut flour and process. Then add the spelt flour. Process for another minute and mix in walnut pieces at the end.

Pour cake batter into a large (8- to 9-inch) springform cake pan. Bake in the oven for 45 minutes or until you can stick a fork in the top and it comes out clean.

To prepare icing, remove the liquid from the coconut milk cans and put the cream in the large, chilled mixing bowl. Using an electric mixer, beat the coconut until it forms a whipped cream. This should take about 30 seconds.

Beat in cacao powder and then dates with the electric mixer. Mix for 30 seconds and then refrigerate.

Frost the cake with the cream and add your favorite toppings. If desired, you can cut the cake in half horizontally and spread icing in the center as well to make it a layer cake.

Ice creams

CHAPTER 5

"The best time for ice cream is always."
— Unknown

You were like a dream,
ice cream.

When my day wasn't
what it could have been.

You made my heart sing,
flutter with an airy thing.

Even if struggles came in other ways,
your refreshing deliciousness perpetually stays.

MINT PISTACHIO ICE CREAM

MAKES
6 SERVINGS

METHOD
FREEZE

PREP TIME
NIGHT BEFORE &
20 MINUTES

COOK TIME
NONE

¾ cup coconut water or
  non-dairy milk

2 frozen bananas

3 medjool dates, pitted

1 teaspoon vanilla bean powder

1 tablespoon fresh mint leaves

1 cup raw pistachio nuts, soaked
  overnight or for at least 4 hours

¼ cup raw pistachio pieces for
  garnish (optional)

Night before: soak pistachios

Place all ingredients, except pistachios, into a high-powered blender. Blend until smooth—you may need to pause and scrape down the sides. Next blend in the soaked pistachios, liquid removed, and blend until smooth again.

Transfer into a freezer-friendly container of your choice. Place in the freezer to chill for at least 4-5 hours or overnight.

Stir every hour for a couple of hours (if you've got the time) for a more even, ice cream-like texture. Scoop out and enjoy.

The ice cream will freeze until solid, so allow it to sit out for 15 minutes or so before serving. For increased pistachio flavor, garnish with pistachio pieces.

You can prepare these ice cream recipes with an ice cream maker or without an ice cream maker. The choice is yours.

If preparing with an ice cream maker, pour the ice cream into the prepared ice cream maker and follow the manufacturer's instructions.

CARAMELIZED PEANUT BUTTER
ICE CREAM

MAKES
6 SERVINGS

METHOD
FREEZE

PREP TIME
NIGHT BEFORE &
5 MINUTES

CHILL TIME
NONE

¾ cup raw cashews, soaked overnight and drained

3 large bananas, frozen

1 cup non-dairy milk of choice

3 tablespoons peanut butter

1 tablespoon cacao powder

5 medjool dates, pitted

1 tablespoon maca powder

1 teaspoon ground vanilla

½ teaspoon cinnamon

Night before: soak cashews

Place all ingredients in a high-powered blender or food processor and slowly process, 15 seconds at a time, until mixture is smooth, uniform and creamy, scraping down the sides as you go.

You can serve it immediately for a soft-serve treat.

For a firmer, scoopable ice cream, transfer it to a sealed, freezer-safe container and store it in the freezer for at least 3 hours (stir once every hour to incorporate air).

STRAWBERRY CASHEW ICE CREAM

MAKES
8 SERVINGS

METHOD
FREEZE

PREP TIME
NIGHT BEFORE &
7-10 MINUTES

CHILL TIME
2 HOURS

---

2 cups raw cashews, soaked in water overnight and drained

½ cup cashew, almond or coconut milk

4 cup fresh ripe or frozen organic strawberries, defrosted

6 medjool dates, pitted

1 teaspoon vanilla bean powder

Night before: soak cashews

Like the majority of these ice cream recipes, you can make them with an ice cream maker or without an ice cream maker.

Without an ice cream maker:
Blend all ingredients in a high-powered blender.

Pour the mixture into a freezer safe container and freeze. Every hour or so, remove from the freezer and stir/whisk to incorporate air. Repeat this until the ice cream is mostly firm. This should take about 6 hours.

Allow the ice cream to sit out for 10-15 minutes before serving.

With an ice cream maker:
Place the bowl of the ice cream maker in the freezer and let it freeze overnight.

Place the cashews in a bowl and soak with non-dairy milk overnight or for at least 4 hours.

Refrigerate the ice cream base until it is cold, about 1-2 hours.

Blend the entire soaked nut mixture until it is creamy. Then add the strawberries, dates and vanilla bean powder and blend until smooth.

Pour the ice cream base into the ice cream maker and follow the manufacturer's instructions. Once the ice cream has finished churning, pour it into a freezer safe container.

Cover and freeze until hard. The ice cream will freeze until solid, so allow it to sit out for 10-15 minutes before serving.

EXPRESSO FUDGE ICE CREAM

MAKES
8 SERVINGS

METHOD
FREEZE

PREP TIME
NIGHT BEFORE &
10 MINUTES

COOK TIME
1 HOUR

¾ cup raw cashews, soaked overnight and drained

1 (15 oz.) can coconut milk, refrigerated overnight, then liquid removed*

1½ cup non-dairy milk (I use cashew milk)

3 heaping tablespoons cocoa powder

1 teaspoon ground coffee of choice

1 teaspoon vanilla bean powder

8 medjool dates, pitted

6 oz. 85% dark chocolate, chopped

2 tablespoons arrowroot

*After refrigeration overnight, the cream will have separated from the liquid. Drain the liquid and set aside, you will use only the cream for this recipe.

Night before: soak cashews, refrigerate coconut milk

In a high-powered blender, combine dates, drained cashews, coconut milk (should be creamy from the can, do not add the liquid part), non-dairy milk, cocoa powder, ground coffee and vanilla and blend until everything is smooth and creamy.

Put one cup of blended mixture to the side. With a saucepan on medium heat, gradually pour the rest of the mixture into the saucepan. Add the dark chocolate to the saucepan and whisk it into the mixture as it melts. Blend the remaining one cup of mixture with the arrowroot until dissolved. Gradually pour mixture from blender into the saucepan and whisk continuously as you do. Once everything is incorporated, whisk until the entire mixture comes to a light boil to cook arrowroot and thicken the mixture. Continue whisking so no lumps form.

Once the mixture starts to boil, turn heat off and transfer into a bowl, cover and cool to room temperature. Once cooled, churn the mixture in an ice cream maker and follow ice cream maker instructions. If you don't have an ice cream maker, you can manually churn the ice cream.

Place in a freezer safe container and freeze. Allow the ice cream to set for a few hours before eating. You may need to let it sit out of the freezer for about 15 minutes before scooping. Use a warm ice cream scoop to make scooping easier.

CHERRY VANILLA ICE CREAM

MAKES
4 SERVINGS

METHOD
CHILL

PREP TIME
NIGHT BEFORE &
1 HOUR

CHILL TIME
5 HOURS

½ cup raw cashews, soaked overnight

¼ cup walnuts

1 cup non-dairy milk of choice

1 ½ teaspoon vanilla bean powder

1 ½ cups fresh or frozen pitted cherries

5 medjool dates, pitted

Night before: soak cashews

Soak cashew nuts in water overnight or for at least 4 hours.

Blend the pitted cherries and softened dates in a food processor or blender until smooth. Then add the soaked nuts along with the milk. Blend until smooth—you may need to pause and scrape down the sides.

Transfer into a freezer-friendly container of your choice. Place in the freezer to chill for at least 4-5 hours or overnight.

Stir every hour for a couple of hours (if you've got the time) for a more even, ice cream-like texture. Leave out for 5-10 minutes before serving.

You can prepare these ice cream recipes with an ice cream maker or without an ice cream maker. The choice is yours.

If preparing with an ice cream maker, pour the ice cream into the prepared ice cream maker and follow the manufacturer's instructions.

MATCHA ICE CREAM BARS

MAKES
16 SERVINGS

METHOD
CHILL

PREP TIME
NIGHT BEFORE &
15 MINUTES

CHILL TIME
5 HOURS

For the base

1 ½ cup raw almonds

5 medjool dates, pitted

½ cup cocoa powder

2 tablespoons maca powder

For the matcha middle layer

2 ½ tablespoons matcha powder (green tea powder)

2 (15 oz.) cans coconut milk, refrigerated overnight, then liquid removed*

¾ cup raw cashews, soaked for at least 5 hours, drained

5 medjool dates, pitted, soaked in water overnight, drained

2 teaspoon vanilla bean powder

For the chocolate top layer

½ cup raw almond butter

½ cup cocoa powder

3 medjool dates, pitted

*After refrigeration overnight, the cream will have separated from the liquid. Drain the liquid and set aside, you will use only the cream for this recipe.

Night before: soak cashews, dates, refrigerate coconut milk

Cover an 8x8 inch baking dish with parchment paper. Set the pan aside.

To prepare the base layer, add the raw almond butter and pitted medjool dates to a food processor and process thoroughly. Once evenly mixed, add cocoa powder and maca powder and process for another minute or until a chocolaty mixture is formed. Transfer into the baking dish, making sure to evenly spread it and smooth the top. Place in the refrigerator while you prepare the middle matcha layer.

To prepare the middle layer, mix the coconut milk, cashews, matcha, medjool dates and vanilla powder in a high-powered blender or food processor until smooth and creamy. Make sure not to add the liquid from the coconut milk cans. Take the pan out of the refrigerator and spread this layer on top of the bottom layer. Smooth the top evenly. Chill in the refrigerator until top layer is complete.

For the top layer, heat the almond butter in the microwave 30 seconds, stir, and then reheat another 20 seconds. Mix this in the food processor with the cacao powder and pitted dates until crumbly. Cover the middle layer with this topping. Chill in the refrigerator for at least one hour before slicing into bars and serving.

For this recipe, use high quality coconut milk. There is a generic kind that is slightly cheaper but doesn't work quite as well and the ice cream will be less creamy. Organic coconut milk is the real trick.

PECAN MANGO SHERBET BARS

MAKES
12 SERVINGS

METHOD
CHILL

PREP TIME
NIGHT BEFORE &
30 MINUTES

CHILL TIME
4 HOURS

Mango sherbet cream base:

3 cups cubed mango (fresh or frozen)

5 slices of dried mango

1 cup non-dairy milk

¼ cup walnuts

1 tablespoon freshly squeezed lemon juice

1 teaspoon vanilla bean powder

For the middle vanilla sherbet cream

1 (15 oz.) can coconut milk, refrigerated overnight, then liquid removed*

1 teaspoon vanilla bean powder

8 medjool dates, pitted

⅓ cup soy milk

Nutella vanilla top layer:

1 ½ cup raw pecans, soaked overnight in warm water

½ cup almond butter

12 medjool dates, pitted

2 teaspoons vanilla bean powder

¾ cup cocoa powder

*After refrigeration overnight, the cream will have separated from the liquid. Drain the liquid and set aside, you will use only the cream for this recipe.

Night before: soak pecans, refrigerate coconut milk

Soak the dried mango, pecans, and dates, if the dates are not soft already. Line an 8x8 inch pan with tin foil or parchment paper. Place the pan in the freezer while you prepare the mango sherbet base. To prepare the mango sherbet, first soak the dried mango in the non-dairy milk for at least 4 hours or overnight. Then place all ingredients in a food processor and process until all ingredients are thoroughly processed. Take the pan out of the freezer and pour in this base layer, smoothing out the top. Place this layer in the freezer while you prepare the middle vanilla cream layer.

To prepare the middle vanilla layer, place all ingredients in cleaned food processor and process until smooth and creamy. Take the pan out of the freezer and add the vanilla cream layer to the top of the mango layer, smoothing out the top. This layer will be thinner and that's okay. Place the pan back in the freezer while preparing the top layer.

Prepare the pecan top layer by first processing the soaked pecans in cleaned food processor. Process completely before adding almond butter, pitted dates and ground vanilla. It also helps if you soak the pitted dates to soften them. Soak dates in water overnight or microwave soaked in water for 30 seconds before removing them from water and adding them to the food processor. Process these ingredients until smooth.

Lastly, add cocoa powder to the food processor and process that in until a smooth, even mixture forms. Take the pan out of the freezer and pour this layer on top of the vanilla layer, smoothing out the top. Freeze for at least 4 hours or overnight. When you are ready to serve them, remove them from the pan, cut into squares, decorate as you please.

The word sherbet has a different meaning than sorbet. Traditional sorbet only contains fruit and sugar—no dairy or cream of any kind. It's often churned in an ice cream maker, which makes it scoop-able but not creamy. Sherbet is halfway between sorbet and ice cream. It is always fruit-based, and I use non-dairy milk or coconut cream.

BERRY SHERBET CUPS

MAKES
8 SERVINGS

METHOD
CHILL

PREP TIME
NIGHT BEFORE &
45 MINUTES

CHILL TIME
1 HOUR

For raspberry sherbet

1 (15 oz.) can coconut milk, refrigerated overnight, then liquid removed*

1 cup fresh or frozen raspberries

1 teaspoon vanilla bean powder

6 medjool dates, pitted

For blackberry sherbet

1 (15 oz.) can coconut milk, refrigerated overnight, then liquid removed*

1 cup fresh or frozen blackberries

2 teaspoons vanilla bean powder

6 medjool dates, pitted

*After refrigeration overnight, the cream will have separated from the liquid. Drain the liquid and set aside, you will use only the cream for this recipe.

Night before: refrigerate coconut milk

Retrieve a muffin tin that can hold at least 8 muffins. You can use muffin liners because they will make it easier to take the sorbet cups out, but I didn't use them and it worked well.

In a high-powered blender, blend all of the raspberry layer ingredients. Then fill 4 of the cups in the muffin tin halfway full and freeze for 15 minutes. Reserve raspberry leftovers in a bowl in the fridge for now. You want to have half of the sherbet cups with the raspberry on the bottom and half with the raspberry on top.

Next blend all of the blackberry layer ingredients until smooth. Pour the blackberry layer on top of the raspberry layer in the 4 cups so that the muffin cups are now full. In the other 4 cups, add the remaining blackberry sherbet, filling the cups halfway up.

Freeze for another 30 minutes (at least) before removing the cups from the freezer and pouring the remaining raspberry leftovers on top of the halfway filled blackberry cups.

Freeze for at least an hour so that the cups can completely harden. Then, using a sharp knife, slowly take them out of the muffin tins. It will get a bit messy, but this is part of the fun. Store leftovers in the freezer.

ALMOND BLACKBERRY
ICE CREAM SQUARES

MAKES
15 SQUARES

METHOD
CHILL

PREP TIME
NIGHT BEFORE &
20 MINUTES

CHILL TIME
6 HOURS

For the crust:

½ cup almond flour

1 cup rolled or old-fashioned oats

1 cup raw almond butter

8 medjool dates, pitted

1 teaspoon vanilla bean powder

For the middle blackberry layer:

½ cup raw cashews, soaked in water overnight or for at least 4 hours

1 cup walnuts, soaked in water overnight or for at least 4 hours

1 teaspoon vanilla bean powder

1 frozen banana, sliced

8 medjool dates, pitted

½ cup non-dairy milk

3 heaping tablespoons blackberry powder

For the top vanilla layer:

1 frozen banana

⅓ cup non-dairy milk

1½ teaspoon vanilla bean powder

6 medjool dates, pitted

⅓ teaspoon cinnamon

Night before: soak cashews, walnuts

To prepare the crust, add almond flour, rolled oats, almond butter and vanilla to a food processor and process until fully combined. Add the dates and process until a nice mixture forms.

Line an 8x8 inch square pan (or one of similar size) with parchment paper and press the crust firmly into it, smoothing the top. Chill the crust in the freezer until the next layer is ready.

To prepare the blackberry middle layer, drain the soaked nuts and process, in your cleaned food processor. Once this is done, process in vanilla, frozen banana, dates, non-dairy milk and blackberry powder until smooth and creamy. Spread this mixture on top of the crust and freeze for 2 hours.

To prepare vanilla top layer, place the frozen bananas in a processor or blender with the almond milk. Then add the other ingredients and blend in. Spread this mixture on top of the blackberry mixture and chill for at least 4 hours before slicing and serving. These bars should be kept in the freezer and can be eaten immediately without defrosting.

The best news about dark chocolate for anyone who loves the sunshine is that it potently protects our skin from damage when exposed to ultraviolet (UV) light from the sun's rays. An antioxidant-rich diet with vegetables and fruit at the base is our greatest insurance against skin cancer, but the flavonoids (a class of antioxidants) in cocoa powder have also been proven to keep our skin smoother, moister and clearer than those who don't eat any dark chocolate.[1]

Spanish explorers arriving in Mexico during the 16th century survived on avocados and were the first Europeans to consume them. As a result of the Spanish Conquest, avocados spread to South America and Central America. Sadly, they had yet to learn how to make avocado toast.

Need to ripen that avocado ASAP? Place it in a brown paper bag with a banana or two. The bananas will release ethylene gas, a natural plant hormone that aids in ripening fruit.

RICH CHOCOLATE MOUSSE

MAKES
6 SERVINGS

METHOD
CHILL

PREP TIME
15 MINUTES

CHILL TIME
6 HOURS

6 medjool dates, pitted

½ cup bittersweet chocolate

⅓ cup cocoa powder

2 ripe avocados

¼ cup your favorite non-dairy milk

1 teaspoon vanilla bean powder

Optional toppings
fresh berries
pomegranates
edible flowers
dried fruits/nuts

Combine all ingredients in a food processor or high-powered blender and blend until smooth and creamy. Store in a container and chill in the refrigerator for at least 15 minutes before serving. Garnish as desired.

In the photo you see the chocolate crust recipe from the Chocolate Crusted Cherry Pie topped with the rich chocolate mousse (page 160).

CHOCOLATE HAZELNUT MILKSHAKE

MAKES
2 SERVINGS

METHOD
CHILL

PREP TIME
15 MINUTES ROASTING,
10 MINUTES PREP

CHILL TIME
2 HOURS

¼ cup whole hazelnuts, soaked in water overnight and drained

¾ cup almond or hemp milk

1 tablespoon ground flaxseeds or chia seeds

2 tablespoons cocoa powder

4 dates, pitted

1 teaspoon vanilla bean powder

8-10 ice cubes

Preheat oven to 350 degrees F.

Toast hazelnuts in oven for 15 minutes. Remove and put on a towel. Rub the nuts with the towel to remove their shells.

Combine all ingredients in a high-powered blender and blend until smooth. Add the ice cubes to create a milkshake-like texture.

For a quicker version, use walnuts instead of hazelnuts because you don't need to toast them. Simply soak walnuts for 1 hour and you are ready to roll.

Hazelnuts generally have the highest proanthocyanidin content of any tree nut. Proanthocyanidin are a type of anthocyanidin.

Anthocyanins have been shown to help dampen allergic reactions and inhibit tumor cells in humans.

Given that hazelnuts possess the highest anthocyanin content of any tree nut, this means that they are a superfood, keeping us young and fighting cancer and heart disease like they mean business.[2,3]

COCOA-NUT DREAM PUDDING

MAKES
5 SERVINGS

METHOD
NONE

PREP TIME
NIGHT BEFORE &
10 MINUTES

CHILL TIME
15 MINUTES

¼ cup grated 85% dark chocolate

1 can coconut milk, refrigerated overnight

⅓ cup raw cashew butter

⅓ cup cacao powder

3 medjool dates, pitted

Night before: refrigerate coconut milk

Heat dark chocolate in the microwave for 30 seconds before adding it to a high-powered blender or food processor.

Remove liquid from refrigerated coconut milk can and add to blender too. Blend all of the ingredients until smooth.

Chill for at least 15 minutes in the fridge before serving.

Pour over your favorite fruit.

For this recipe, use high quality coconut milk. There is a generic kind that is slightly cheaper but doesn't work quite as well and the ice cream will be less creamy. Organic coconut milk is the real trick.

STRAWBERRY PINEAPPLE SORBET

MAKES
2 SERVINGS

METHOD
CHILL

PREP TIME
NIGHT BEFORE &
10 MINUTES

CHILL TIME
2 HOURS

¼ cup or 4 slices dried, unsweetened, unsulfured pineapple

¼ cup orange juice

10 ounces frozen strawberries (one bag)

1 navel orange, peeled or one cup frozen pineapple

Fruit toppings of choice (optional)

¼ cup shredded coconut (optional)

Night before: soak pineapple

Soak dried pineapple in orange juice until softened: overnight or at least two hours. Blend dried pineapple and soaking juice, frozen strawberries and the orange (or frozen pineapple) in a high-powered blender until smooth.

Pour into sorbet glasses and top with sliced fresh strawberries and/or other desired fruit toppings and shredded coconut, if desired. Freeze to your desired consistency.

CHOCOLATE FUDGSICLE POPS

MAKES
6 SERVINGS

METHOD
CHILL

PREP TIME
10 MINUTES

CHILL TIME
2 HOURS

2 ripe bananas

½ cup raw cashews or raw
   cashew butter

½ cup raw walnuts

3 tablespoons cocoa powder

1 teaspoon vanilla bean powder

5 medjool dates, pitted

2 tablespoons non-dairy milk

Blend ingredients together in a food processor or high-powered blender until smooth.

Spoon into an ice pop tray and freeze for at least 2 hours before serving. Rinse outside of trays with hot water to pull the pops out easily.

Note: You can also blend in 1 cup of frozen strawberries, blueberries or cherries.

MATCHA CREAM SMOOTHIE

MAKES
3 SERVINGS

METHOD
BLEND

PREP TIME
15 MINUTES

CHILL TIME
NONE

For the smoothie

2 frozen bananas

2 teaspoons ground flaxseeds

2 medjool dates, pitted

10 ice cubes + ¼ cup water

1 tablespoon matcha powder

1 teaspoon vanilla bean powder

Handful of raw spinach

**For the chocolate
swirl topping**

2 tablespoons almond butter

1 small ripe banana

2 heaping tablespoons cocoa
   powder

1 cup almond milk

2 medjool dates

Place all smoothie ingredients in a blender and mix until smooth and creamy. Pour into a bowl.

For the chocolate swirl topping, place ingredients in a high-powered blender and blend until smooth and creamy. Scoop a few tablespoons of the chocolate mixture with a spoon into the matcha smoothie bowl. Use the tip of a sharp knife to make swirls on top of the smoothie.

Add toppings, as desired such as shredded coconut, pomegranates, hazelnuts, matcha powder, cocoa powder, chia seeds and a few edible flowers.

STRAWBERRY KALE SMOOTHIE

MAKES
2 SERVINGS

METHOD
BLEND

PREP TIME
15 MINUTES

CHILL TIME
NONE

1 ½ cup frozen strawberries, defrosted

2 frozen bananas

1 Pitaya Plus smoothie pack (for additional pink hue, optional)*

2 medjool dates, pitted

⅓ cup non-dairy milk of choice

1 teaspoon vanilla bean powder

½ cup raw kale

1 teaspoon ground flaxseeds

1 teaspoon ground chia seeds

1 teaspoon raw hemp seeds

Optional toppings
fresh berries
nuts
seeds
granola
edible flowers

*Note: Pitaya is another word for dragon fruit. Pitaya Plus is the brand I use and can be found on Amazon and in many health food stores. Using them in smoothies will result in a pinker treat.

Blend strawberries, bananas, pitaya (if using), dates, vanilla and milk in a high-powered blender until all ingredients are smooth and creamy.

Then add the kale and blend.

Pour into a large bowl and stir with seeds.

VANILLA ICE CREAM SMOOTHIE BOWL

MAKES
5 SERVINGS

METHOD
REFRIGERATE

PREP TIME
NIGHT BEFORE &
5 MINUTES

COOK TIME
NONE

---

1 (15 oz.) can coconut milk, refrigerated overnight, then liquid removed*

½ cup walnuts, soaked overnight in non-dairy milk

2 bananas, frozen

5 medjool dates, pitted

1 ½ teaspoon vanilla bean powder

Optional toppings

fresh berries

pomegranates

melted dark chocolate

cranberries

edible flowers

*After refrigeration overnight, the cream will have separated from the liquid. Drain the liquid and set aside, you will use only the cream for this recipe.

Night before: soak walnuts, refrigerate coconut milk

The night before, refrigerate a can of coconut milk and soak walnuts in non-dairy milk. A mason jar is great for soaking nuts overnight.

The next day, drain walnuts, discarding liquid, then place all ingredients (including coconut cream) in a food processor or high-powered blender and process/blend until smooth and creamy.

Pour into a large bowl or two smaller ones, top with your favorite toppings or serve over steel cut oats and berries.

209

BROWNIE SMOOTHIE BOWL

MAKES
4 SERVINGS

METHOD
CHILL

PREP TIME
10 MINUTES

CHILL TIME
2 HOURS

½ ripe avocado

2 frozen bananas

¼ cup cocoa powder

4 medjool dates, pitted

1 heaping tablespoon chia seeds

2 teaspoons vanilla bean
    powder

½ cup non-dairy milk

Optional toppings
cacao nibs
dark chocolate chunks
your favorite nuts and/or seeds
fresh berries

Simply blend or process all ingredients until completely combined. Pour into 4 serving glasses and place in the fridge.

Chill them for at least 2 hours to firm up or overnight for best results.

Once chilled, remove from the fridge and sprinkle with optional toppings.

Chia seeds are a rich source of essential omega-3 fatty acids, and they pack in protein. About 23 percent of the calories in chia seeds come from protein.

Bonus, they make you feel satiated. Chia seeds are high in soluble fiber, which is why they form a thick gel when mixed with water and set aside for 30 minutes. Research indicates that this reaction also occurs in the stomach, slowing the process in which digestive enzymes break down carbohydrates and convert them to sugar. A slower digestive process leads to feelings of fullness in the stomach for a long period of time.

STRAWBERRY COCONUT
SMOOTHIE BOWL

MAKES
4 SERVINGS

METHOD
NONE

PREP TIME
NIGHT BEFORE &
5-10 MINUTES

CHILL TIME
NONE

- 1 (15 oz) can coconut milk, refrigerated overnight, then liquid removed*
- 3 frozen bananas
- 2 cups organic strawberries (fresh or frozen, defrosted)
- 1 teaspoon ground vanilla
- 2 tablespoons chia seeds
- 1 pitaya smoothie pack from Pitaya Plus** (optional, for color)

Optional toppings
assorted berries
nuts
seeds
oats
dark chocolate

*After refrigeration overnight, the cream will have separated from the liquid. Drain the liquid and set aside, you will use only the cream for this recipe.

Night before: refrigerate coconut milk

Blend together all ingredients in a high-powered blender or food processor. Make sure to use only the top creamy portion of the can of refrigerated coconut milk.

Once completely blended, pour into two or three bowls and decorate with your favorite toppings.

Numerous studies have found that berries significantly reduce our risk of heart disease in a way no other food group can. What is it about berries that literally enables them to love our hearts? The deep red, blue and purple pigments of berries are produced by flavonoid antioxidant molecules called anthocyanins, which are concentrated in the skins of the fruits.[4]

**To purchase pitaya smoothie pack, head to pitayaplus.com or you can find pitaya (also known as dragon fruit) in many health food stores.

SUMMER LOVERS SMOOTHIE BOWL

MAKES
2 SERVINGS

METHOD
NONE

PREP TIME
10 MINUTES

CHILL TIME
NONE

1 banana (frozen)

½ cup organic strawberries (frozen)

½ cup organic pineapple (frozen)

1 teaspoon flaxseeds

1 teaspoon chia seeds

½ cup non-dairy milk

3 medjool dates, pitted

1 teaspoon ground vanilla

1 pitaya smoothie pack from Pitaya Plus* (optional, for color)

Optional toppings

pineapple

kiwi

fresh berries

shredded coconut

chocolate chips

Place all smoothie ingredients in a high-speed blender or food processor. Blend until smooth.

Spoon the smoothie into a bowl and top with any of your favorite optional toppings.

*To purchase pitaya smoothie pack, head to pitayaplus.com or you can find pitaya (also known as dragon fruit) in many health food stores.

NUTRITION FACTS
COOKIES AND TRUFFLES

Ladyfinger Cookies

Yield: 26 cookies (serving size: 2 cookies)

Per serving: calories 188; protein 5g; carbohydrates 36g; sugars 18g; total fat 4.6g; saturated fat 0.8g; sodium 9mg; fiber 4.2g; beta-carotene 23ug; vitamin c 2mg; calcium 58mg; iron 1.6mg; folate 19ug; magnesium 90mg; potassium 409mg; zinc 1.2mg; selenium 3ug

Unclassic Chocolate Cookies

Yield 14 cookies (serving size: 1 cookie)

Per serving: calories 165; protein 5g; carbohydrates 32g; sugars 15g; total fat 4.1g; saturated fat 0.7g; sodium 101mg; fiber 4.6g; beta-carotene 21ug; vitamin c 9mg; calcium 76mg; iron 1.8mg; folate 15ug; magnesium 64mg; potassium 412mg; zinc 0.9mg; selenium 5.9ug

Maca Chocolate Chip Cookies

Yield: 14 cookies (serving size: 1 cookie)

Per serving: calories 216; protein 5g; carbohydrates 36g; sugars 18g; total fat 7.1g; saturated fat 2.8g; cholesterol 0.3mg; sodium 7mg; fiber 4.6g; beta-carotene 22ug; vitamin c 4mg; calcium 74mg; iron 2.5mg; folate 18ug; magnesium 71mg; potassium 426mg; zinc 1.2mg; selenium 7.2ug

Peanut Butter Bliss Cookie

Yield: 15 cookies (serving size: 1 cookie)

Per serving: calories 203; protein 5g; carbohydrates 24g; sugars 16g; total fat 11.1g; saturated fat 2.6g; cholesterol 0.2mg; sodium 71mg; fiber 3.6g; beta-carotene 18ug; calcium 49mg; iron 1.4mg; folate 18ug; magnesium 62mg; potassium 348mg; zinc 0.9mg; selenium 3ug

Raspberry Jam Thumbprint Cookies

Yield: 15 cookies (serving size : 1 cookie)

Per serving: calories 255; protein 5g; carbohydrates 35g; sugars 20g; total fat 12.2g; saturated fat 5.4g; sodium 3mg; fiber 6.1g; beta-carotene 24ug; vitamin c 6mg; calcium 89mg; iron 5mg; folate 17ug; magnesium 70mg; potassium 325mg; zinc 1mg; selenium 5.7ug

Nutsy Chocolate Chip Cookies

Yield: 18 cookies (serving size: 1 cookie)

Per serving: calories 198; protein 5g; carbohydrates 31g; sugars 15g; total fat 7.4g; saturated fat 0.8g; sodium 9mg; fiber 4g; beta-carotene 19ug; vitamin c 1mg; calcium 75mg; iron 1.4mg; folate 26ug; magnesium 60mg; potassium 365mg; zinc 1mg; selenium 7.3ug

Lemon Cookies

Yield: 16 cookies (serving size: 1 cookie)

Per serving: calories 156; protein 4g; carbohydrates 25g; sugars 14g; total fat 5.8g; saturated fat 0.8g; sodium 51mg; fiber 3g; beta-carotene 19ug; vitamin c 1mg; calcium 58mg; iron 1mg; folate 13ug; magnesium 53mg; potassium 257mg; zinc 0.8mg; selenium 4.1ug

Pumpkin Spice Cookies

Yield: 14 cookies (serving size: 1 cookie)

Per serving: calories 325; protein 9g; carbohydrates 55g; sugars 20g; total fat 9.1g; saturated fat 2.6g; cholesterol 0.2mg; sodium 19mg; fiber 6.9g; beta-carotene 2133ug; vitamin c 1mg; calcium 109mg; iron 4.1mg; folate 24ug; magnesium 109mg; potassium 549mg; zinc 1.9mg; selenium 15.1ug

Banana Oat Cookies

Yield: 15 cookies (serving size: 1 cookie)

Per serving: calories 165; protein 4g; carbohydrates 30g; sugars 17g; total fat 4.5g; saturated fat 0.6g; sodium 4mg; fiber 3.7g; beta-carotene 21ug; vitamin c 2mg; calcium 52mg; iron 2.3mg; folate 13ug; magnesium 47mg; potassium 332mg; zinc 0.6mg; selenium 3.1ug

Green Tea Cookies

Yield: 22 cookies (serving size: 2 cookies)

Per serving: calories 277; protein 6g; carbohydrates 49g; sugars 23g; total fat 8.7g; saturated fat 2.1g; sodium 19mg; fiber 4.8g; beta-carotene 29ug; vitamin c 5mg; calcium 107mg; iron 2.2mg; folate 20ug; magnesium 82mg; potassium 592mg; zinc 1.4mg; selenium 7.5ug

Sweet Potato Spice Cookies

Yield: 15 cookies (serving size: 1 cookie)

Per serving: calories 131; protein 4g; carbohydrates 18g; sugars 8g; total fat 6g; saturated fat 0.5g; sodium 92mg; fiber 2.9g; beta-carotene 2074ug; vitamin c 3mg; calcium 63mg; iron 0.9mg; folate 10ug; magnesium 47mg; potassium 267mg; zinc 0.6mg; selenium 2.4ug

Spiced Walnut Cookies

Yield: 10 cookies (serving size: 1 cookie)

Per serving: calories 267; protein 6g; carbohydrates 38g; sugars 19g; total fat 11.9g; saturated fat 5.4g; sodium 11mg; fiber 4.4g; beta-carotene 35ug; calcium 75mg; iron 1.5mg; folate 15ug; magnesium 67mg; potassium 387mg; zinc 1.1mg; selenium 9.1ug

Strawberry Shortcake Cookies

Yield: 14 cookies (serving size: 1 cookie)

Per serving: calories 191; protein 5g; carbohydrates 30g; sugars 14g; total fat 6.8g; saturated fat 0.7g; sodium 12mg; fiber 4.2g; beta-carotene 20ug; vitamin c 8mg; calcium 100mg; iron 1.4mg; folate 17ug; magnesium 66mg; potassium 370mg; zinc 1mg; selenium 6.4ug

Flourless Almond Ginger Cookies

Yield: 17 cookies (serving size: 1 cookie)

Per serving: calories 292; protein 3g; carbohydrates 38g; sugars 28g; total fat 17g; saturated fat 12.1g; sodium 5mg; fiber 4g; beta-carotene 38ug; vitamin c 1mg; calcium 100mg; iron 0.9mg; folate 12ug; magnesium 44mg; potassium 466mg; zinc 0.4mg; selenium 0.3ug

Ice Cream Scoop Cookies

Yield: 10 cookies (serving size: 1 cookie)

Per serving: calories 286; protein 9g; carbohydrates 45g; sugars 18g; total fat 10g; saturated fat 3.1g; cholesterol 0.1mg; sodium 7mg; fiber 6.6g; beta-carotene 23ug; calcium 91mg; iron 2.4mg; folate 41ug; magnesium 93mg; potassium 536mg; zinc 1.5mg; selenium 13.4ug

Pecan Raisin Cookies

Yield: 9 cookies (serving size: 1 cookie)

Per serving: calories 254; protein 7g; carbohydrates 45g; sugars 21g; total fat 6.9g; saturated fat 0.9g; sodium 10mg; fiber 6g; beta-carotene 1317ug; vitamin c 6mg; calcium 68mg; iron 2.2mg; folate 50ug; magnesium 59mg; potassium 452mg; zinc 1.2mg; selenium 6.3ug

Peanut Butter Espresso Truffles

Yield: 9 truffles (serving size: 1 truffle)

Per serving: calories 162; protein 3g; carbohydrates 26g; sugars 20g; total fat 6.7g; saturated fat 2.5g; cholesterol 0.2mg; sodium 3mg; fiber 3.8g; beta-carotene 25ug; calcium 28mg; iron 1.6mg; folate 10ug; magnesium 55mg; potassium 358mg; zinc 0.7mg; selenium 1.2ug

Matcha Cashew Truffles

Yield: 8 truffles (serving size: 1 truffle)

Per serving: calories 153; protein 4g; carbohydrates 21g; sugars 16g; total fat 7.3g; saturated fat 1.1g; sodium 2mg; fiber 2.3g; beta-carotene 22ug; calcium 29mg; iron 1mg; folate 15ug; magnesium 68mg; potassium 283mg; zinc 1mg; selenium 1ug

BROWNIES, BLONDIES AND BARS

Peanut Butter Black Bean Brownies

Yield: 8 brownies (serving size: 1 brownie)

Per serving: calories 258; protein 9g; carbohydrates 48g; sugars 25g; total fat 7.7g; saturated fat 1.8g; sodium 164mg; fiber 10.3g; beta-carotene 32ug; calcium 84mg; iron 3mg; folate 69ug; magnesium 123mg; potassium 698mg; zinc 1.8mg; selenium 5ug

Triple Layer Bars

Yield: 16 bars (serving size: 1 bar)

Per serving: calories 253; protein 6g; carbohydrates 40g; sugars 25g; total fat 10.4g; saturated fat 2.2g; sodium 8mg; fiber 5g; beta-carotene 35ug; vitamin c 1mg; calcium 65mg; iron 1.7mg; folate 22ug; magnesium 89mg; potassium 463mg; zinc 1.3mg; selenium 4.5ug

Almond Mocha Bars

Yield: 15 bars (serving size: 1 bar)

Per serving: calories 198; protein 3g; carbohydrates 38g; sugars 28g; total fat 6g; saturated fat 1.4g; sodium 10mg; fiber 4.2g; beta-carotene 38ug; vitamin c 4mg; calcium 64mg; iron 1.8mg; folate 15ug; magnesium 58mg; potassium 430mg; zinc 0.8mg; selenium 1.3ug

Coconut Blueberry Squares

Yield: 12 bars (serving size: 1 bar)

Per serving: calories 239; protein 6g; carbohydrates 43g; sugars 18g; total fat 6.8g; saturated fat 2.3g; sodium 12mg; fiber 5.9g; beta-carotene 28ug; vitamin c 3mg; calcium 86mg; iron 2mg; folate 22ug; magnesium 84mg; potassium 482mg; zinc 1.4mg; selenium 18.1ug

Cashew Butter Fudge

Yield: 15 bars (serving size: 1 bar)

Per serving: calories 346; protein 9g; carbohydrates 43g; sugars 24g; total fat 18.3g; saturated fat 4.8g; cholesterol 0.1mg; sodium 7mg; fiber 6.8g; beta-carotene 32ug; vitamin c 1mg; calcium 53mg; iron 3.3mg; folate 53ug; magnesium 111mg; potassium 588mg; zinc 1.9mg; selenium 4.3ug

Goji Berry Blondies

Yield: 12 blondies (serving size: 1 blondie)

Per serving: calories 291; protein 8g; carbohydrates 31g; sugars 8g; total fat 17.9g; saturated fat 5g; sodium 15mg; fiber 6.4g; beta-carotene 309ug; vitamin c 5mg; calcium 100mg; iron 3mg; folate 25ug; magnesium 94mg; potassium 347mg; zinc 1.7mg; selenium 7.3ug

Strawberry Bliss Brownies

Yield: 20 brownies (serving size: 1 brownie)

Per serving: calories 148; protein 3g; carbohydrates 23g; sugars 15g; total fat 6.7g; saturated fat 4.1g; sodium 5mg; fiber 3.8g; beta-carotene 79ug; vitamin c 5mg; calcium 46mg; iron 1.6mg; folate 15ug; magnesium 41mg; potassium 277mg; zinc 0.5mg; selenium 1.5ug

Double-Decker Fig Brownies

Yield: 15 brownies (serving size: 1 brownie)

Per serving: calories 248; protein 4g; carbohydrates 40g; sugars 26g; total fat 11.7g; saturated fat 2.1g; sodium 88mg; fiber 7.5g; beta-carotene 39ug; vitamin c 2mg; calcium 66mg; iron 3mg; folate 23ug; magnesium 82mg; potassium 596mg; zinc 1mg; selenium 1.9ug

Tahini Brownies

Yield: 16 brownies (serving size: 1 brownie)

Per serving: calories 192; protein 5g; carbohydrates 35g; sugars 19g; total fat 7.2g; saturated fat 1.6g; sodium 6mg; fiber 6.7g; beta-carotene 36ug; vitamin c 3mg; calcium 124mg; iron 2.4mg; folate 22ug; magnesium 93mg; potassium 712mg; zinc 1.6mg; selenium 4.6ug

Cashew Cream Lemon Bars

Yield: 16 bars (serving size: 1 bar)

Per serving: calories 237; protein 4g; carbohydrates 31g; sugars 21g; total fat 12.6g; saturated fat 6.6g; sodium 6mg; fiber 3.4g; beta-carotene 27ug; vitamin c 4mg; calcium 41mg; iron 3mg; folate 15ug; magnesium 68mg; potassium 370mg; zinc 1mg; selenium 1.8ug

Peanut Butter Blondies

Yield: 16 blondies (serving size: 1 blondie)

Per serving: calories 174; protein 5g; carbohydrates 27g; sugars 16g; total fat 6.7g; saturated fat 1g; sodium 81mg; fiber 3.6g; beta-carotene 21ug; vitamin c 1mg; calcium 34mg; iron 3mg; folate 22ug; magnesium 35mg; potassium 280mg; zinc 0.5mg; selenium 0.9ug

Oatmeal Butterscotch Blondies

Yield: 16 blondies (serving size: 1 blondie)

Per serving: calories 325; protein 9g; carbohydrates 49g; sugars 19g; total fat 11.4g; saturated fat 1.4g; sodium 12mg; fiber 7.2g; beta-carotene 26ug; vitamin c 2mg; calcium 109mg; iron 2.3mg; folate 38ug; magnesium 74mg; potassium 505mg; zinc 1.1mg; selenium 8.9ug

Chocolate Sweet Potato Squares

Yield: 15 squares (serving size: 1 square)

Per serving: calories 325; protein 6g; carbohydrates 61g; sugars 38g; total fat 9.4g; saturated fat 4.1g; cholesterol 0.3mg; sodium 15mg; fiber 9.3g; beta-carotene 3546ug; vitamin c 6mg; calcium 70mg; iron 4.9mg; folate 32ug; magnesium 102mg; potassium 761mg; zinc 1.3mg; selenium 2.2ug

Raspberry Chocolate Frozen Bars

Yield: 20 bars (serving size: one bar)

Per serving: calories 338; protein 9g; carbohydrates 35g; sugars 20g; total fat 22g; saturated fat 5.1g; sodium 5mg; fiber 7.4g; beta-carotene 28ug; vitamin c 6mg; calcium 59mg; iron 3.1mg; folate 37ug; magnesium 131mg; potassium 681mg; zinc 2.2mg; selenium 4.6ug

Fudgy Avo Bars

Yield: 15 bars (serving size: one bar)

Per serving: calories 178; protein 4g; carbohydrates 35g; sugars 24g; total fat 4.9g; saturated fat 0.7g; sodium 6mg; fiber 5.7g; beta-carotene 97ug; vitamin c 3mg; calcium 56mg; iron 1.9mg; folate 24ug; magnesium 60mg; potassium 466mg; zinc 0.7mg; selenium 1.2ug

Raspberry Chocolate Bars

Yield: 16 bars (serving size: one bar)

Per serving: calories 345; protein 6g; carbohydrates 38g; sugars 23g; total fat 21.5g; saturated fat 9.5g; sodium 11mg; fiber 5.6g; beta-carotene 32ug; vitamin c 7mg; calcium 58mg; iron 3.3mg; folate 33ug; magnesium 92mg; potassium 493mg; zinc 1.5mg; selenium 4.5ug

Breakfast Superfood Kale Bars

Yield: 12 bars (serving size: one bar)

Per serving: calories 297; protein 9g; carbohydrates 37g; sugars 18g; total fat 15.2g; saturated fat 3.4g; sodium 24mg; fiber 6g; beta-carotene 537ug; vitamin c 8mg; calcium 94mg; iron 3.7mg; folate 30ug; magnesium 72mg; potassium 403mg; zinc 1.1mg; selenium 4.4ug

Matcha Marathon Squares

Yield: 16 squares (serving size: one square)

Per serving: calories 136; protein 3g; carbohydrates 25g; sugars 16g; total fat 3.7g; saturated fat 0.6g; sodium 2mg; fiber 2.5g; beta-carotene 21ug; vitamin c 7mg; calcium 24mg; iron 2.2mg; folate 15ug; magnesium 43mg; potassium 292mg; zinc 0.6mg; selenium 0.9ug

BREAD AND MUFFINS

Chocolate Peanut Butter Bread

Yield: 12 slices (serving size: 1 slice)

Per serving: calories 274; protein 7g; carbohydrates 50g; sugars 29g; total fat 8.3g; saturated fat 1.6g; sodium 7mg; fiber 7.1g; beta-carotene 40ug; vitamin c 3mg; calcium 94mg; iron 2.3mg; folate 26ug; magnesium 101mg; potassium 718mg; zinc 1.4mg; selenium 6.9ug

Raspberry Vanilla Bread

Yield: 12 slices (serving size: 1 slice)

Per serving: calories 227; protein 5g; carbohydrates 46g; sugars 24g; total fat 3.5g; saturated fat 0.4g; sodium 115mg; fiber 6g; beta-carotene 32ug; vitamin c 5mg; calcium 82mg; iron 1.5mg; folate 31ug; magnesium 65mg; potassium 482mg; zinc 1mg; selenium 13.9ug

Pumpkin Dough Bread

Yield 12 slices (serving size: 1 slice)

Per serving: calories 285; protein 7g; carbohydrates 52g; sugars 25g; total fat 7.4g; saturated fat 2.2g; cholesterol 0.2mg; sodium 20mg; fiber 7.6g; beta-carotene 1144ug; vitamin c 2mg; calcium 94mg; iron 6.5mg; folate 47ug; magnesium 66mg; potassium 528mg; zinc 0.9mg; selenium 1.9ug

Coconut Banana Bread

Yield: 12 servings

Per serving: calories 229; protein 6g; carbohydrates 37g; sugars 18g; total fat 7.9g; saturated fat 1g; sodium 14mg; fiber 5g; beta-carotene 26ug; vitamin c 3mg; calcium 129mg; iron 1.7mg; folate 22ug; magnesium 80mg; potassium 531mg; zinc 1.2mg; selenium 7.2ug

Zucchini Bread

Yield 12 slices (serving size: 1 slice)

Per serving: calories 247; protein 6g; carbohydrates 44g; sugars 20g; total fat 6.4g; saturated fat 0.9g; sodium 115mg; fiber 5.2g; beta-carotene 68ug; vitamin c 6mg; calcium 84mg; iron 1.9mg; folate 25ug; magnesium 76mg; potassium 516mg; zinc 1.5mg; selenium 10.8ug

Chai Spice Cornbread

Yield: 11 muffins (serving size: 1 muffin)

Per serving: calories 294; protein 6g; carbohydrates 52g; sugars 28g; total fat 9.4g; saturated fat 1.5g; sodium 137mg; fiber 6g; beta-carotene 2145ug; vitamin c 4mg; calcium 117mg; iron 2.8mg; folate 26ug; magnesium 91mg; potassium 624mg; zinc 1.3mg; selenium 3.6ug

Apple Pie Muffins

Yield: 10 muffins (serving size: 1 muffin)

Per serving: calories 289; protein 6g; carbohydrates 52g; sugars 32g; total fat 8.8g; saturated fat 1g; sodium 12mg; fiber 7g; beta-carotene 45ug; vitamin c 6mg; calcium 142mg; iron 1.7mg; folate 30ug; magnesium 89mg; potassium 635mg; zinc 1.2mg; selenium 9.2ug

Tropical Carrot Cake Muffins

Yield: 12 muffins (serving size: 1 muffin)

Per serving: calories 318; protein 5g; carbohydrates 45g; sugars 26g; total fat 15.4g; saturated fat 12.4g; sodium 21mg; fiber 5.6g; beta-carotene 1182ug; vitamin c 2mg; calcium 91mg; iron 2.7mg; folate 24ug; magnesium 68mg; potassium 584mg; zinc 1.1mg; selenium 10.5ug

Peanut Butter and Jelly Muffins

Yield: 16 muffins (serving size: 1 muffin)

Per serving: calories 229; protein 5g; carbohydrates 39g; sugars 20g; total fat 8g; saturated fat 1g; sodium 6mg; fiber 4.6g; beta-carotene 22ug; vitamin c 2mg; calcium 72mg; iron 1.3mg; folate 30ug; magnesium 60mg; potassium 421mg; zinc 1mg; selenium 10.7ug

Caramel Chocolate Chip Muffins

Yield: 12 muffins (serving size: 1 muffin)

Per serving: calories 294; protein 6g; carbohydrates 50g; sugars 26g; total fat 9.4g; saturated fat 3.4g; cholesterol 0.3mg; sodium 125mg; fiber 6.1g; beta-carotene 34ug; vitamin c 6mg; calcium 102mg; iron 3.1mg; folate 27ug; magnesium 96mg; potassium 575mg; zinc 1.5mg; selenium 8.9ug

Lemon Poppy Seed Muffins

Yield: 12 muffins (serving size: 1 muffin)

Per serving: calories 184; protein 5g; carbohydrates 33g; sugars 16g; total fat 5.6g; saturated fat 0.5g; sodium 2mg; fiber 4.9g; beta-carotene 22ug; vitamin c 1mg; calcium 109mg; iron 2.8mg; folate 15ug; magnesium 57mg; potassium 363mg; zinc 0.8mg; selenium 6.9ug

Superfood Chocolate Muffins

Yield: 16 muffins (serving size: 1 muffin)

Per serving: calories 299; protein 10g; carbohydrates 57g; sugars 24g; total fat 6.4g; saturated fat 3.1g; sodium 3mg; fiber 10.8g; beta-carotene 31ug; vitamin c 1mg; calcium 81mg; iron 3.4mg; folate 76ug; magnesium 85mg; potassium 658mg; zinc 1.1mg; selenium 2.3ug

Sunflower Coconut Muffins
Yield: 15 muffins (serving size: 1 muffin)
Per serving: calories 168; protein 4g; carbohydrates 28g; sugars 16g; total fat 6.4g; saturated fat 2.4g; sodium 9mg; fiber 4.1g; beta-carotene 23ug; vitamin c 8mg; calcium 79mg; iron 1.1mg; folate 26ug; magnesium 53mg; potassium 381mg; zinc 0.7mg; selenium 7.5ug

Macadamia Ginger Pear Muffins
Yield: 10 muffins (serving size: 1 muffin)
Per serving: calories 283; protein 6g; carbohydrates 55g; sugars 29g; total fat 6.5g; saturated fat 0.8g; sodium 3mg; fiber 8.3g; beta-carotene 39ug; vitamin c 3mg; calcium 100mg; iron 1.8mg; folate 24ug; magnesium 62mg; potassium 509mg; zinc 0.9mg; selenium 8.9ug

Blueberry Banana Muffins
Yield: 12 muffins (serving size: 1 muffin)
Per serving: calories 205; protein 5g; carbohydrates 37g; sugars 20g; total fat 6.3g; saturated fat 1.2g; sodium 6mg; fiber 5.3g; beta-carotene 33ug; vitamin c 3mg; calcium 76mg; iron 1.4mg; folate 32ug; magnesium 73mg; potassium 459mg; zinc 0.9mg; selenium 9.4ug

Chocolate Dream Muffins
Yield: 14 muffins (serving size: 1 muffin)
Per serving: calories 165; protein 4g; carbohydrates 35g; sugars 16g; total fat 3.3g; saturated fat 0.7g; sodium 12mg; fiber 4.7g; beta-carotene 23ug; vitamin c 2mg; calcium 46mg; iron 4.6mg; folate 10ug; magnesium 42mg; potassium 341mg; zinc 0.5mg; selenium 1.1ug

Chocolate Beet Muffins
Yield: 8 muffins (serving size: 1 muffin)
Per serving: calories 312; protein 7g; carbohydrates 57g; sugars 30g; total fat 10.4g; saturated fat 5.3g; sodium 14mg; fiber 9.1g; beta-carotene 51ug; vitamin c 15mg; calcium 117mg; iron 3.8mg; folate 43ug; magnesium 104mg; potassium 823mg; zinc 1.3mg; selenium 11.2ug

Superfood Berry Muffins
Yield: 8 muffins (serving size: 1 muffin)
Per serving: calories 287; protein 7g; carbohydrates 55g; sugars 31g; total fat 6.9g; saturated fat 2g; sodium 5mg; fiber 8g; beta-carotene 37ug; vitamin c 5mg; calcium 117mg; iron 1.8mg; folate 45ug; magnesium 83mg; potassium 690mg; zinc 1.2mg; selenium 10.9ug

PIES, CAKES AND TORTES

Angel Food Layer Cake
Yield: 18 servings
Per serving: calories 306; protein 5g; carbohydrates 34g; sugars 22g; total fat 19.3g; saturated fat 10.4g; sodium 14mg; fiber 3.7g; beta-carotene 29ug; vitamin c 1mg; calcium 88mg; iron 3.9mg; folate 23ug; magnesium 88mg; potassium 499mg; zinc 1.2mg; selenium 1.7ug

Coconut Cream Tiramisu
Yield: 14 servings
Per serving: calories 321; protein 5g; carbohydrates 31g; sugars 18g; total fat 21.1g; saturated fat 14.1g; sodium 15mg; fiber 3.7g; beta-carotene 21ug; vitamin c 2mg; calcium 39mg; iron 2.2mg; folate 24ug; magnesium 81mg; potassium 451mg; zinc 1.4mg; selenium 7.9ug

Dark Chocolate Jewel Cake
Yield: 12 servings
Per serving: calories 289; protein 6g; carbohydrates 47g; sugars 33g; total fat 14.1g; saturated fat 8.3g; sodium 12mg; fiber 7.8g; beta-carotene 44ug; vitamin c 5mg; calcium 68mg; iron 3.9mg; folate 24ug; magnesium 124mg; potassium 708mg; zinc 1.6mg; selenium 2.5ug

Strawberry Ice Cream Cake
Yield: 18 servings
Per serving: calories 338; protein 6g; carbohydrates 59g; sugars 43g; total fat 13g; saturated fat 7g; sodium 15mg; fiber 7.9g; beta-carotene 63ug; vitamin c 8mg; calcium 84mg; iron 3.2mg; folate 50ug; magnesium 104mg; potassium 789mg; zinc 1.3mg; selenium 1.7ug

Chocolate Coffee Cake
Yield: 10 servings
Per serving: calories 299; protein 10g; carbohydrates 62g; sugars 36g; total fat 6.5g; saturated fat 1.7g; sodium 140mg; fiber 12.3g; beta-carotene 47ug; calcium 113mg; iron 4.7mg; folate 88ug; magnesium 136mg; potassium 968mg; zinc 1.8mg; selenium 2.9ug

Nut-Free Chocolate Cake
Yield: 12 servings
Per serving: calories 239; protein 3g; carbohydrates 34g; sugars 25g; total fat 14g; saturated fat 11.5g; sodium 6mg; fiber 5.5g; beta-carotene 33ug; vitamin c 10mg; calcium 43mg; iron 2.2mg; folate 12ug; magnesium 68mg; potassium 531mg; zinc 0.8mg; selenium 1.4ug

Pineapple Carrot Cake

Yield: 16 servings

Per serving: calories 290; protein 5g; carbohydrates 33g; sugars 21g; total fat 17.9g; saturated fat 11.2g; sodium 20mg; fiber 4.8g; beta-carotene 886ug; vitamin c 12mg; calcium 101mg; iron 3.9mg; folate 21ug; magnesium 64mg; potassium 460mg; zinc 0.7mg; selenium 0.6ug

Pumpkin Butter Layer Cake

Yield: 14 servings

Per serving: calories 302; protein 6g; carbohydrates 39g; sugars 25g; total fat 16.3g; saturated fat 9.4g; sodium 17mg; fiber 5.2g; beta-carotene 639ug; vitamin c 5mg; calcium 74mg; iron 3mg; folate 30ug; magnesium 90mg; potassium 551mg; zinc 1.2mg; selenium 4.2ug

Peanut Butter Pie

Yield: 15 servings

Per serving: calories 297; protein 7g; carbohydrates 39g; sugars 26g; total fat 15.8g; saturated fat 4g; sodium 4mg; fiber 5g; beta-carotene 23ug; vitamin c 2mg; calcium 94mg; iron 13.3mg; folate 44ug; magnesium 74mg; potassium 434mg; zinc 1.1mg; selenium 2.9ug

Pistachio Cream Cake

Yield: 20 servings

Per serving: calories 335; protein 7g; carbohydrates 39g; sugars 25g; total fat 20.4g; saturated fat 10.6g; sodium 7mg; fiber 5.3g; beta-carotene 44ug; vitamin c 1mg; calcium 50mg; iron 3.2mg; folate 33ug; magnesium 107mg; potassium 590mg; zinc 1.7mg; selenium 2.8ug

Half-Baked Strawberry Cake

Yield: 16 servings

Per serving: calories 318; protein 5g; carbohydrates 43g; sugars 28g; total fat 18g; saturated fat 13.3g; sodium 15mg; fiber 6.1g; beta-carotene 44ug; vitamin c 12mg; calcium 93mg; iron 3.1mg; folate 23ug; magnesium 91mg; potassium 648mg; zinc 1.2mg; selenium 3.9ug

Berry Mango Rainbow Cake

Yield: 10 servings

Per serving: calories 268; protein 3g; carbohydrates 32g; sugars 26g; total fat 16.4g; saturated fat 11.7g; sodium 11mg; fiber 4g; beta-carotene 86ug; vitamin c 12mg; calcium 46mg; iron 2.8mg; folate 26ug; magnesium 60mg; potassium 449mg; zinc 0.7mg; selenium 0.6ug

Fall Spice Cake

Yield 12 servings

Per serving: calories 246; protein 6g; carbohydrates 50g; sugars 23g; total fat 4.9g; saturated fat 0.5g; sodium 13mg; fiber 6.9g; beta-carotene 34ug; vitamin c 4mg; calcium 99mg; iron 3.4mg; folate 30ug; magnesium 62mg; potassium 543mg; zinc 0.9mg; selenium 2.9ug

Gingerbread Layer Cake

Yield: 22 servings

Per serving: calories 344; protein 7g; carbohydrates 37g; sugars 18g; total fat 20.9g; saturated fat 10.6g; sodium 11mg; fiber 4.4g; beta-carotene 26ug; vitamin c 2mg; calcium 77mg; iron 2mg; folate 38ug; magnesium 92mg; potassium 476mg; zinc 1.5mg; selenium 5.9ug

Pistachio Chocolate Cream Pie

Yield: 18 servings

Per serving: calories 325; protein 8g; carbohydrates 38g; sugars 26g; total fat 19.1g; saturated fat 9.4g; sodium 7mg; fiber 7.5g; beta-carotene 59ug; vitamin c 2mg; calcium 51mg; iron 3mg; folate 38ug; magnesium 132mg; potassium 625mg; zinc 1.8mg; selenium 4.7ug

Chocolate Crusted Cherry Pie

Yield: 24 servings

Per serving: calories 346; protein 7g; carbohydrates 45g; sugars 29g; total fat 18.3g; saturated fat 5.4g; sodium 5mg; fiber 4.4g; beta-carotene 40ug; vitamin c 3mg; calcium 79mg; iron 8.2mg; folate 27ug; magnesium 108mg; potassium 508mg; zinc 1.8mg; selenium 3.4ug

Raw Ice Cream Cake

Yield: 18 servings

Per serving: calories 319; protein 7g; carbohydrates 35g; sugars 24g; total fat 19.6g; saturated fat 7.9g; sodium 7mg; fiber 4.5g; beta-carotene 29ug; vitamin c 8mg; calcium 52mg; iron 3.2mg; folate 21ug; magnesium 122mg; potassium 522mg; zinc 1.9mg; selenium 5ug

Vanilla Blueberry Cheesecake

Yield: 18 servings

Per serving: calories 340; protein 6g; carbohydrates 46g; sugars 32g; total fat 18.1g; saturated fat 8.7g; sodium 10mg; fiber 6.8g; beta-carotene 46ug; vitamin c 3mg; calcium 66mg; iron 2.9mg; folate 29ug; magnesium 103mg; potassium 602mg; zinc 1.6mg; selenium 3.9ug

Tropical Cream Pie
Yield: 14 servings
Per serving: calories 271; protein 4g; carbohydrates 36g; sugars 26g; total fat 14.8g; saturated fat 7g; sodium 8mg; fiber 4.4g; beta-carotene 145ug; vitamin c 11mg; calcium 44mg; iron 2.2mg; folate 29ug; magnesium 74mg; potassium 466mg; zinc 1.1mg; selenium 3.4ug.

Chocolate Avo Torte
Yield: 9 servings
Per serving: calories 218; protein 6g; carbohydrates 40g; sugars 21g; total fat 6.3g; saturated fat 1.3g; sodium 3mg; fiber 8.6g; beta-carotene 46ug; vitamin c 7mg; calcium 42mg; iron 2mg; folate 50ug; magnesium 74mg; potassium 529mg; zinc 0.9mg; selenium 2.6ug.

Raspberry Lovin' Torte
Yield: 10 servings
Per serving: calories 344; protein 7g; carbohydrates 39g; sugars 25g; total fat 21g; saturated fat 11.3g; sodium 10mg; fiber 5.8g; beta-carotene 35ug; vitamin c 4mg; calcium 87mg; iron 3.7mg; folate 30ug; magnesium 95mg; potassium 508mg; zinc 1.1mg; selenium 2.1ug.

Walnut Rum Mocha Cake
Yield: 16 servings
Per serving: calories 320; protein 6g; carbohydrates 40g; sugars 22g; total fat 17.8g; saturated fat 11.3g; sodium 10mg; fiber 5.9g; beta-carotene 30ug; vitamin c 1mg; calcium 75mg; iron 3.7mg; folate 22ug; magnesium 90mg; potassium 561mg; zinc 1.2mg; selenium 1.6ug.

ICE CREAMS AND SMOOTHIES

Mint Pistachio Ice Cream
Yield: 6 servings
Per serving: calories 191; protein 5g; carbohydrates 25g; sugars 15g; total fat 9.5g; saturated fat 1.2g; sodium 32mg; fiber 4.3g; beta-carotene 72ug; vitamin c 5mg; calcium 39mg; iron 1.1mg; folate 21ug; magnesium 50mg; potassium 512mg; zinc 0.6mg; selenium 2.1ug.

Caramelized Peanut Butter Ice Cream
Yield: 6 servings
Per serving: calories 286; protein 7g; carbohydrates 41g; sugars 24g; total fat 13g; saturated fat 2.2g; sodium 36mg; fiber 4.9g; beta-carotene 36ug; vitamin c 14mg; calcium 118mg; iron 2.5mg; folate 33ug; magnesium 106mg; potassium 668mg; zinc 1.6mg; selenium 5.1ug.

Strawberry Cashew Ice Cream
Yield: 8 servings
Per serving: calories 301; protein 8g; carbohydrates 35g; sugars 19g; total fat 16.8g; saturated fat 2.9g; sodium 19mg; fiber 4.8g; beta-carotene 46ug; vitamin c 46mg; calcium 75mg; iron 3.6mg; folate 31ug; magnesium 133mg; potassium 538mg; zinc 2.4mg; selenium 8.2ug.

Expresso Fudge Ice Cream
Yield: 8 servings
Per serving: calories 356; protein 6g; carbohydrates 36g; sugars 22g; total fat 23.1g; saturated fat 13.1g; cholesterol 0.6mg; sodium 47mg; fiber 5.1g; beta-carotene 25ug; calcium 136mg; iron 5.2mg; folate 13ug; magnesium 129mg; potassium 551mg; zinc 1.9mg; selenium 4.3ug.

Cherry Vanilla Ice Cream
Yield: 4 servings
Per serving: calories 249; protein 5g; carbohydrates 35g; sugars 27g; total fat 11.8g; saturated fat 1.8g; sodium 3mg; fiber 3.9g; beta-carotene 331ug; vitamin c 1mg; calcium 39mg; iron 1.9mg; folate 18ug; magnesium 81mg; potassium 423mg; zinc 1.4mg; selenium 3.7ug.

Matcha Ice Cream Bars
Yield 16 servings
Per serving: calories 306; protein 8g; carbohydrates 27g; sugars 15g; total fat 22.2g; saturated fat 8.4g; sodium 8mg; fiber 5.7g; beta-carotene 18ug; vitamin c 6mg; calcium 95mg; iron 3.7mg; folate 22ug; magnesium 130mg; potassium 607mg; zinc 1.7mg; selenium 2.5ug.

Pecan Mango Sherbet Bars
Yield: 12 servings
Per serving: calories 340; protein 5g; carbohydrates 45g; sugars 34g; total fat 19.4g; saturated fat 6.1g; sodium 23mg; fiber 7.1g; beta-carotene 309ug; vitamin c 16mg; calcium 113mg; iron 2.6mg; folate 36ug; magnesium 97mg; potassium 613mg; zinc 1.5mg; selenium 1.9ug.

Berry Sherbet Cups
Yield: 8 servings
Per serving: calories 299; protein 3g; carbohydrates 34g; sugars 27g; total fat 19.1g; saturated fat 16.8g; sodium 12mg; fiber 4.4g; beta-carotene 47ug; vitamin c 5mg; calcium 48mg; iron 3.5mg; folate 27ug; magnesium 68mg; potassium 497mg; zinc 0.8mg; selenium 0.1ug.

Almond Blackberry Ice Cream Squares

Yield: 15 servings

Per serving: calories 336; protein 8g; carbohydrates 41g; sugars 27g; total fat 18.1g; saturated fat 1.7g; sodium 8mg; fiber 6.3g; beta-carotene 36ug; vitamin c 2mg; calcium 112mg; iron 3.1mg; folate 28ug; magnesium 106mg; potassium 517mg; zinc 1.3mg; selenium 2ug

Rich Chocolate Mousse

Yield: 6 servings

Per serving: calories 318; protein 5g; carbohydrates 44g; sugars 31g; total fat 18.2g; saturated fat 6.6g; sodium 7mg; fiber 10.1g; beta-carotene 75ug; vitamin c 18mg; calcium 38mg; iron 1.9mg; folate 45ug; magnesium 90mg; potassium 730mg; zinc 1.2mg; selenium 1.6ug

Chocolate Hazelnut Milkshake

Yield: 2 servings

Per serving: calories 290; protein 5g; carbohydrates 45g; sugars 33g; total fat 13.5g; saturated fat 1.3g; sodium 73mg; fiber 7.4g; beta-carotene 45ug; vitamin c 1mg; calcium 246mg; iron 2.5mg; folate 32ug; magnesium 100mg; potassium 682mg; zinc 1.2mg; selenium 2ug

Cocoa-Nut Dream Pudding

Yield: 5 servings

Per serving: calories 315; protein 6g; carbohydrates 24g; sugars 12g; total fat 24.9g; saturated fat 14.9g; cholesterol 0.3mg; sodium 13mg; fiber 4.1g; beta-carotene 14ug; vitamin c 1mg; calcium 40mg; iron 4.7mg; folate 24ug; magnesium 126mg; potassium 466mg; zinc 1.9mg; selenium 3.4ug

Strawberry Pineapple Sorbet

Yield: 2 servings

Per serving: calories 154; protein 2g; carbohydrates 40g; sugars 26g; total fat 0.5g; sodium 5mg; fiber 6.1g; beta-carotene 149ug; vitamin c 169mg; calcium 71mg; iron 1.5mg; folate 77ug; magnesium 40mg; potassium 510mg; zinc 0.4mg; selenium 1.1ug

Chocolate Fudgsicle Pops

Yield: 6 servings

Per serving: calories 280; protein 6g; carbohydrates 33g; sugars 18g; total fat 16.6g; saturated fat 2.9g; sodium 5mg; fiber 4.2g; beta-carotene 29ug; vitamin c 4mg; calcium 35mg; iron 2mg; folate 35ug; magnesium 104mg; potassium 502mg; zinc 1.7mg; selenium 3.6ug

Matcha Cream Smoothie

Yield: 3 servings

Per serving: calories 293; protein 6g; carbohydrates 56g; sugars 36g; total fat 8.4g; saturated fat 0.9g; sodium 75mg; fiber 8g; beta-carotene 620ug; vitamin c 13mg; calcium 243mg; iron 2.1mg; folate 57ug; magnesium 117mg; potassium 967mg; zinc 1.1mg; selenium 2.4ug

Strawberry Kale Smoothie

Yield: 2 servings

Per serving: calories 266; protein 5g; carbohydrates 59g; sugars 36g; total fat 3.4g; saturated fat 0.5g; sodium 18mg; fiber 8.5g; beta-carotene 1628ug; vitamin c 76mg; calcium 77mg; iron 2.2mg; folate 61ug; magnesium 95mg; potassium 870mg; zinc 0.8mg; selenium 3.4ug

Vanilla Ice Cream Smoothie Bowl

Yield: 5 servings

Per serving: calories 289; protein 4g; carbohydrates 32g; sugars 22g; total fat 18.8g; saturated fat 11.4g; sodium 8mg; fiber 3.5g; beta-carotene 35ug; vitamin c 5mg; calcium 38mg; iron 2.5mg; folate 31ug; magnesium 68mg; potassium 507mg; zinc 0.8mg; selenium 1ug

Brownie Smoothie Bowl

Yield: 4 servings

Per serving: calories 208; protein 5g; carbohydrates 39g; sugars 24g; total fat 6.2g; saturated fat 1.5g; sodium 8mg; fiber 8.1g; beta-carotene 57ug; vitamin c 12mg; calcium 45mg; iron 1.6mg; folate 36ug; magnesium 81mg; potassium 607mg; zinc 0.9mg; selenium 2.8ug

Strawberry Coconut Smoothie Bowl

Yield: 4 servings

Per serving: 282; protein 4g; carbohydrates 32g; sugars 14g; total fat 17.7g; saturated fat 13.7g; sodium 13mg; fiber 6.3g; beta-carotene 43ug; vitamin c 39mg; calcium 74mg; iron 3.7mg; folate 40ug; magnesium 89mg; potassium 613mg; zinc 1mg; selenium 5.3ug

Summer Lovers Smoothie Bowl

Yield 2 servings

Calories 235; protein 3g; carbohydrates 54g; sugars 38g; total fat 3g; saturated fat 0.3g; sodium 51mg; fiber 7.2g; beta-carotene 77ug; vitamin c 48mg; calcium 181mg; iron 1.5mg; folate 38ug; magnesium 71mg; potassium 671mg; zinc 0.6mg; selenium 2.8ug

SCIENTIFIC REFERENCES

INTRODUCTION — ENJOY GOOD HEALTH

1. Starr VL, Convit A: Diabetes, sugar-coated but harmful to the brain. Curr Opin Pharmacol 2007, 7:638-642.

2. Kodl CT, Seaquist ER: Cognitive dysfunction and diabetes mellitus. Endocr Rev 2008, 29:494-511.

3. Starr VL, Convit A: Diabetes, sugar-coated but harmful to the brain. Curr Opin Pharmacol 2007, 7:638-642.

4. Kodl CT, Seaquist ER: Cognitive dysfunction and diabetes mellitus. Endocr Rev 2008, 29:494-511.

5. Kroner Z: The relationship between Alzheimer's disease and diabetes: Type 3 diabetes? Altern Med Rev 2009, 14:373-379.

6. Shariff M, Quik M, Holgate J, et al. Neuronal Nicotinic Acetylcholine Receptor Modulators Reduce Sugar Intake. PLOS ONE. 2016;11(3): e0150270; Klenowski PM, Shariff MR, Belmer A, et al. Prolonged Consumption of Sucrose in a Binge-Like Manner, Alters the Morphology of Medium Spiny Neurons in the Nucleus Accumbens Shell. Frontiers in Behavioral Neuroscience. 2016;10:54.

7. Yang Q, Zhang Z, Gregg EW, et al. Added sugar intake and cardiovascular diseases mortality among US adults. JAMA Intern Med. April 2014;174(4):516-24.

8. Janssens J. How nutrition during the first few decades of life affects breast cancer risk implications for research and dietary guidelines for children. Nutrition Today Sept 1999; Hilakivi-Clarke E, Cho S, deAssis S, et al. Maternal and prepubertal diet, mammary development and breast cancer risk J Nutr 2001;131:154S–157S; Pike MC, Henderson BE. Casagrande JT IN: Pike MC, Siiten PK, Welsh CN, eds. Hormones and cancer. New York, Banbury Reports, Cold Springs Harbor Laboratory 3, 1981.

9. McPherson K, Steel CM, Dixon JM. ABC of Breast Diseases, Breast cancer—epidemiology, risk factors, and genetics. BMJ 2000;321:624–628. Pierce DA, Shimizu Y, Preston DL, et al. Studies of the mortality of atomic bomb survivors. Report 12, Part I. Cancer:1950–1990 RERF Report No. 11–95. Radiat Res 1996;146:1–27; Tsuji K, Harashima, E, Nakagawa Y, et al. Time-lag effect of dietary fiber and fat intake ratio on Japanese colon cancer mortality. Biomed Environ 1996;9(2–3):223–8; "Maynard M, Gunnell D, Emmett P, et al. Fruit, vegetable and antioxidants in childhood and risk of adult cancer: the Boyd Orr cohort. J Epidemiol Community Health 2003;57:218–225 ; M, Gunnell D, Emmett P, et al. Fruit, vegetable and antioxidants in childhood and risk of adult cancer: the Boyd Orr cohort. J Epidemiol Community Health 2003;57:218–225.

10. Al-Shahib W and Marshall RJ. The fruit of the date palm: its possible use as the best food for the future? Int J Food Sci Nutr,

54(4):247{259, 2003; Rock W, Rosenblat M, Borochov-Neori H, Volkova N, Judeinstein S, Elias M and Aviram M. Effects of date (Phoenix dactylifera L., Medjool or Hallawi Variety) consumption by healthy subjects on serum glucose and lipid levels and on serum oxidative status: a pilot study. J. Agric. Food. Chem. 2009;57(17):8010-8017.

11. Hammouda H, Cherif JK, Trabeisi-Ayadi M, et al. Detailed Polyphenol and Tannin Composition and Its Variability in Tunisian Dates (Phoenix dactylifera L.) at Different Maturity Stages. J. Agric. Food Chem., 2013, 61 (13), pp 3252–3263.

12. Frankel S, Gunnel DJ, Peters TJ, et al., "Childhood Energy Intake and Adult Mortality from Cancer," British Medical Journal 316, no. 7130 (1998):499–504.

13. Sieri S, Krogh V, Berrino F, et al., "Dietary Glycemic Load and Index and Risk of Coronary Heart Disease in a Large Italian Cohort: The EPICOR Study," Archives of Internal Medicine 170, no. 7 (2010): 640–47.

14. Salmeron J, Manson JE, Stampfer MJ, et al. Dietary fiber, glycemic load, and risk of non-insulin-dependent diabetes mellitus in women. JAMA 1997, 277:472-477.

15. Barclay AW, Petocz P, McMillan-Price J, et al., "Glycemic Index, Glycemic Load, and Chronic Disease Risk—A Meta-Analysis of Observational Studies," American Journal of Clinical Nutrition 87, no. 3 (2008):627–37.

16. Newby PK et al., "Dietary Patterns and Changes in Body Mass Index and Waist Circumference in Adults," American Journal of Clinical Nutrition 77, no. 6 (2003): 1417–25.

CHAPTER ONE — COOKIES & TRUFFLES

1. Percival SS, Heuvel JPV, Nieves CJ, et al. Bioavailability of herbs and spices in humans as determined by ex vivo inflammatory suppression and DNA strand breaks. J Am Coll Nutr. 2012;31(4):288 - 294. Aggarwal BB, Gupta SC, Sung B. Curcumin: An orally bioavailable blocker of TNF and other pro-inflammatory biomarkers. Br. J. Pharmacol. 2013;169(8):1672 -92. Zhang L,Fiala M, Cashman J, et al. Curcuminoids enhance amyloid-beta uptake by macrophages of Alzheimer's disease patients. J Alzheimers Dis. 2006;10(1):1-7.

2. Li MJ, Yin YC, Wang J, Jiang YF. Green tea compounds in breast cancer prevention and treatment. World J Clin Oncol 2014;5(3): 520–528. Gonzales GF. Ethnobiology and Ethnopharmacology of Lepidium meyenii (Maca), a Plant from the Peruvian Highlands. Evid Based Complement Alternat Med. 2012:193496.

3. Akhtar S, Ismail T, Riaz M. Flaxseed - a miraculous defense against some critical maladies. Pak J Pharm Sci. 2013;26(1):199-

208. Rodriguez-Leyva D, Weighell W, Edel AL, et al. Potent antihypertensive action of dietary flaxseed in hypertensive patients. Hypertension 2013;62(6):1081-9.

4. Hannum SM. Potential impact of strawberries on human health: A review of the science," Critical Reviews in Food Science and Nutrition 2004;44(1):1–17.

CHAPTER TWO — BROWNIES, BLONDIES & BARS

1. Hein S, Whyte AR, Wood E, Rodriguez-Mateos A, Williams CM. Systematic Review of the Effects of Blueberry on Cognitive Performance as We Age. J Gerontol A Biol Sci Med Sci 2019, 74:984-995.

2. McCann SE, Thompson LU, Nie J, et al: Dietary lignan intakes in relation to survival among women with breast cancer: the Western New York Exposures and Breast Cancer (WEB) Study. Breast Cancer Res Treat 2010;122:229-235.

CHAPTER THREE — BREADS & MUFFINS

1. Ueshima H, Stamler J, Elliott P, et al., Food Omega-3 Fatty Acid Intake of Individuals (Total, Linolenic Acid, Long-Chain) and Their Blood Pressure, Hypertension 2007;50(2):313–19.

2. Blanco-Diaz MT, Del Rio-Celestino M, Martinez-Valdivieso D, et al. Use of visible and near-infrared spectroscopy for predicting antioxidant compounds in summer squash (Cucurbita pepo ssp pepo). Food Chem. 2014 Dec 1;164:301-8.

3. Hamissou M, Smith AC, Carter E Jr., et al. Antioxidative properties of bitter gourd (Momordica charantia) and zucchini (Cucurbita pepo). Emirates Journal of Food and Agriculture; Al-Ain25.9 (Sep 2013): 641-647.

4. Platt ID, Josse AR, Kendall CW, Jenkins DJ, El-Sohemy A. Postprandial effects of almond consumption on human osteoclast precursors–an ex vivo study. Metabolism. 2011 Jul;60(7):923-9.

5. Hull S, Re R, Chambers L, Echaniz A, Wickham SM. A mid-morning snack of almonds generates satiety and appropriate adjustment of subsequent food intake in healthy women. Eur J Nutr. 2015 Aug;54(5):803-10.

6. Kim Y, Keogh JB, Clifton PM. Benefits of Nut Consumption on Insulin Resistance and Cardiovascular Risk Factors: Multiple Potential Mechanisms of Actions. Nutrients 2017, 9. Kelly JH Jr, Sabate J. Nuts and coronary heart disease: an epidemiological perspective. Br J Nutr. 2006 Nov;96 Suppl 2:S61-7.2006.

7. Butler LT, Vauzour D, Williams CM, et al., "Blueberry-Induced Changes in Spatial Working Memory Correlate with Changes in Hippocampal CREB Phosphorylation and Brain-Derived Neurotrophic Factor (BDNF) Levels," Elsevier 2008;45(30;295–305.

8. Adams LS, Seeram NP, Aggarwal BB, et al: Pomegranate juice, total pomegranate ellagitannins, and punicalagin suppress inflammatory cell signaling in colon cancer cells. Journal of Agricultural and Food Chemistry 2006;54:980-985. Aviram M, Rosenblat M, Gaitini D, et al: Pomegranate juice consumption for 3 years by patients with carotid artery stenosis reduces common carotid intima-media thickness, blood pressure and LDL oxidation. Clin Nutr 2004;23:423-433. Aviram M, Dornfeld L. Pomegranate juice consumption inhibits serum angiotensin converting enzyme activity and reduces systolic blood pressure. Atherosclerosis 2001;158:195-198. Ropacki SA, Patel SM, Hartman RE: Pomegranate Supplementation Protects against Memory Dysfunction after Heart Surgery: A Pilot Study. Evid Based Complement Alternat Med 2013;2013:932401. Bookheimer SY, Renner BA, Ekstrom A, et al. Pomegranate juice augments memory and FMRI activity in middle-aged and older adults with mild memory complaints. Evid Based Complement Alternat Med 2013:946298.

9. Toi M, Bando H, Ramachandran C, et al: Preliminary studies on the anti-angiogenic potential of pomegranate fractions in vitro and in vivo. Angiogenesis 2003;6:121-128. Sartippour MR, Seeram NP, Rao JY, et al. Ellagitannin-rich pomegranate extract inhibits angiogenesis in prostate cancer in vitro and in vivo. Int J Oncol 2008;32:475-480; Adams LS, Zhang Y, Seeram NP, et al. Pomegranate ellagitannin-derived compounds exhibit antiproliferative and antiaromatase activity in breast cancer cells in vitro. Cancer Prev Res 2010;3:108-113.

CHAPTER FOUR — PIES, CAKES & TORTES

1. Abraham K, Friederike W, Lindtner O, et al. Toxicology and risk assessment of coumarin: focus on human data. Mol Nutr Food Res. 2010 Feb;54(2):228-39. doi: 10.1002/mnfr.200900281.

2. Lake BG, Coumarin metabolism, toxicity and carcinogenicity: relevance for human risk assessment. Food Chem Toxicol. 1999 Apr;37(4):423-53. doi: 10.1016/s0278-6915(99)00010-1.

3. Trautwein EA, Vermeer MA, Hiemstra H, et al. LDL-Cholesterol Lowering of Plant Sterols and Stanols - Which Factors Influence Their Efficacy? Nutrients. 2018 Sep; 10(9): 1262.

4. Plant sterols/stanols as cholesterol lowering agents: A meta-analysis of randomized controlled trials. Food Nutr Res. 2008; 52: 10.3402/fnr.v52i0.1811.

5. Shaghaghi MA, Abumweis SS, Jones PJH. Cholesterol-lowering efficacy of plant sterols/stanols provided in capsule and tablet formats: results of a systematic review and meta-analysis. J Acad Nutr Diet. 2013 Nov;113(11):1494-503. doi: 10.1016/j.jand.2013.07.006.

6. Aiyer HS, Vadhanam MV, Stoyanova R, et al., Dietary berries and ellagic acid prevent oxidative DNA damage and modulate expression of DNA repair genes. International Journal of Molecular Science 2008;9(3):327–41.

7. Seeram NP, Momin RA, Nair MG, et al., "Cyclooxygenase inhibitory and antioxidant cyanidin glycosides in cherries and berries. Phytomedicine2001;8:362–69. McCune LM, Kubota C, Stendell-Hollis NR, et al., Cherries and Health: A Review. Critical Reviews in Food Science and Nutrition 2011;51:1–12.

8. J. Beekwilder, R. D. Hall, and C. H. de Vos, "Identification and Dietary Relevance of Antioxidants from Raspberry," Biofactors 23, no. 4 (2005): 197–205. PMID:16498206.

9. J. P. Rauha, S. Remes, M. Heinonen, et al., "Antimicrobial Effects of Finnish Plant Extracts Containing Flavonoids and Other Phenolic Compounds," International Journal of Food Microbiology 56, no. 1 (2000): 3–12. PMID:13810.

10. S. Y. Wang and H. S. Lin, "Antioxidant Activity in Fruits and Leaves of Blackberry, Raspberry, and Strawberry Varies with Cultivar and Developmental Stage," Journal of Agricultural and Food Chemistry 48, no. 2 (2000): 140–46. PMID:13820.

11. M. Liu, X. Q. Li, C. Weber, et al., "Antioxidant and Antiproliferative Activities of Raspberries," Journal of Agricultural and Food Chemistry 50, no. 10 (2002): 2926–30.

12. P. Tate, J. God, R. Bibb, Q. Lu, and L. L. Larcom, "Inhibition of Metalloproteinase Activity by Fruit Extracts," Cancer Letters 212, no. 2 (2004): 153–58. PMID:15279895.

13. Beekwilder J, Hall RD, de Vos CH. Identification and dietary relevance of antioxidants from raspberry. Biofactors 2005;23(4):197–205. Wang Sy, Lin HS. Antioxidant activity in fruits and leaves of blackberry, raspberry, and strawberry varies with cultivar and developmental stage. Journal of Agricultural and Food Chemistry 2000;48(2):140–46. Liu M, Li XQ, Weber C, et al., Antioxidant and antiproliferative activities of raspberries. Journal of Agricultural and Food Chemistry 2002;50(10):2926–30.

CHAPTER FIVE —
ICE CREAMS & SMOOTHIES

1. Williams S, Tamburic S, Lally C. Eating chocolate can significantly protect the skin from UV light. J of Cosmetic Dermatology 2009;8(3):169-173. Ibiebele TI, van der Pols JC, Hughes MC, et al. Dietary pattern in association with squamous cell carcinoma of the skin: a prospective study. Am J Clin Nutr 2007;85(5):1401-8.

2. Bolling BW, McKay DL, Blumberg JB. The phytochemical composition and antioxidant actions of tree nuts. Asia Pac J Clin Nutr. Author manuscript; available in PMC 2016 Sep 6.

3. Bolling BW, Chen CO, McKay DL, et al. Tree nut phytochemicals: composition, antioxidant capacity, bioactivity, impact factors. A systematic review of almonds, Brazils, cashews, hazelnuts, macadamias, pecans, pine nuts, pistachios and walnuts. Nutr Res Rev. 2011 Dec;24(2):244-75. 2013;127:188-196.

4. Cassidy A, Mukamal KJ, Liu L, et al. High anthocyanin intake is associated with a reduced risk of myocardial infarction in young and middle-aged women. Circulation 2013;127:188-196.